P9-CFJ-197

HENRIK IBSEN

WORLD DRAMATISTS

HENRIK IBSEN

HANS GEORG MEYER

TRANSLATED BY HELEN SEBBA

With halftone illustrations

FREDERICK UNGAR PUBLISHING CO.
NEW YORK

Translated from the original German
and published by arrangement with Friedrich Verlag
Velber, Hannover

Copyright © 1972 by Frederick Ungar Publishing Co., Inc.
Printed in the United States of America
Designed by Edith Fowler
Library of Congress Catalog Card Number: 72-163145
ISBN: 0-8044-2616-3 (cloth)

CONTENTS

1-171227

CHRONOLOGY

1828   March 20: Henrik Ibsen is born in Skien, the second son of a family of five boys and one girl. His father, Knud Ibsen (1797–1877), a well-to-do businessman who came from a Danish family of shipowners, was a temperamental, sociable, life-loving man, given to extravagance, sudden rages, and drunkenness. Ibsen's mother, Marichen Altenburg (1799–1869), who came from a wealthy merchant family, was a sensitive, timid woman with a tendency to melancholy and meditative pietism. From the beginning the marriage was an unhappy one. (The parents ultimately separated in 1865.)

1836   Ibsen's father goes bankrupt. The family moves to its last remaining property, a farm in Venstöb, returning to Skien in 1843. Ibsen has to leave school. The experience of being déclassé will have significant consequences for him.

1844   Ibsen is apprenticed to a pharmacist in Grimstadt in the hope that later he may be able to study medicine. He lives in this little town of 800 inhabitants until 1850, studying at night for the university entrance examination.

1846 A servant girl at least ten years older than Ibsen (who is eighteen) bears his illegitimate son, whom he supports until 1860.

1848 Inspired by the revolutionary events in Europe, Ibsen begins his first play, *Catiline*, completed in 1849 and published (by Ibsen himself) in 1850 under the pseudonym Brynjolf Bjarme. *Catiline* (*Catalina*) was first performed on February 24, 1896, in Oslo.

1850 Spring: Ibsen moves to Oslo. Although he does not pass all subjects of the university entrance examination, he is allowed to begin the study of medicine. He becomes associated with revolutionary groups and with the labor movement. September 26: First performance of *The Warrior's Barrow* (*Kjæmpehøien*) in Oslo. Published in 1854.

1851 Ibsen's lifelong—though stormy—friendship with Björnson begins. With Paul Botten-Hansen and Aasmund Vinje he founds the satirical weekly *Andhrimner*, which survives for only nine months and in which the play *Norma* is serialized.

November: Ole Bull invites Ibsen to become stage director of the Norwegian National Theater, founded by Bull in Bergen. Ibsen will hold this position, where he is responsible for staging all plays in the theater's repertoire, until 1857, producing more than a hundred plays whose authors include Eugène Scribe, Shakespeare, Ludvig Holberg, Adam Gottlob Œhlenschlaeger, and Gunnar Heiberg. He is also required to write and rehearse one play a year, to be performed on January 2, the anniversary of the founding of the National Theater. These plays were to form the basis of a national Norwegian repertory.

1852 To study stagecraft, Ibsen visits Copenhagen, where he meets Gunnar Heiberg, and Dresden, where he meets the actors Karl Devrient and Bogumil Dawison.

1853 January 2: First performance of *Midsummer Night* (*Sancthansnatten*) in Bergen.

1855 January 2: First performance of *Lady Inger of Ostrat* (*Fru Inger til Østråt*) in Bergen.

1856 January 2: First performance of *The Feast at Solhaug* (*Gildet på Solhaug*) in Bergen.

1857 January 2: First performance of *Olaf Liljekrans* in Bergen.
Summer: *The Vikings of Helgeland* (*Hærmændene på Helgeland*) finished. Published in 1858. Ibsen is appointed stage director of the Norske Teatret in Oslo, a company that was vigorously challenging the Danish tradition of the Christiania Theater in Oslo. Ibsen's years at the Norske Teatret, where he will remain until 1862, are among the gloomiest of his life. His inadequate salary is extremely confining, and since the theater is run on purely commercial lines, he can produce little but popular drama. He neglects his duties and is subjected to humiliating criticism from the directors.

1858 Ibsen marries Susannah Thoresen ("exactly the sort of character I need—illogical but with a strong poetic instinct. She has great breadth of mind, and her hatred of all petty concerns is almost unbridled").

1859 December 23: Ibsen's only legitimate child, his son Sigurd, is born. (Sigurd Ibsen, who became a high-ranking government official, died in 1930.)
January: *Love's Comedy* (*Kjærlighedens komedie*) published. First performance: November 24, 1873, in Oslo. The Norske Teatret goes bankrupt. Ibsen becomes "artistic adviser" to the Christiania Theater.

1863 *The Pretenders* (*Kongsemnerne*) published. First performance: January 17, 1864. After two unsuccessful applications Ibsen is awarded a traveling grant of 400 talers by the Ministry of Culture.

1864 Ibsen goes by way of Copenhagen, Berlin, and Vienna to Rome, where he lives for four years. Except for brief visits to Scandinavia in 1874 and 1885, he lives abroad until 1891—in Rome, Dresden, and Munich. He spends many summers in Colle Isarco (then Gossensass in Austria) and in Berchtesgaden.

1866 *Brand* published in Copenhagen. First performance: March 24, 1885, Stockholm.

1867 *Peer Gynt* published in Copenhagen. First performance: February 24, 1876, Oslo.

1868 Ibsen moves to Dresden, where he will live until 1875.

1869 *The Young Men's League* (*De unges forbund*) published in Copenhagen.

1871   *Digte*, a volume of poems.

1873   *The Emperor and the Galilean* (*Kejser og Galilæer*) published in Copenhagen. First performance: December 5, 1896, Leipzig.

1875   Ibsen goes to live in Munich.

1877   *The Pillars of Society* (*Samfundets støtter*) published in Copenhagen. First performance: November 14, 1877, Odense.

1878   *The Pillars of Society* produced in Germany. In late autumn Ibsen returns to Rome, where he will live until 1885, except for a year (1879–1880) in Munich.

1879   *A Doll's House* (*Et dukkehjem*) published. First performance: December 21, 1879, Copenhagen. The play arouses passionate—and mixed—reactions. Ibsen is obliged to modify the ending for the first German performance.

1881   *Ghosts* (*Gengangere*). First performance: May, 1882, in Chicago, by a Norwegian traveling company. The first German performance, which arouses an even more violent controversy than *A Doll's House*, takes place on April 14, 1886, in Augsburg, before an invited audience. (Many of Ibsen's plays were first performed privately.) The Freie Bühne opens with it in 1889, and in 1891 it is the first play performed by the London Independent Theater. (Both of these theaters are modeled on the Paris Théâtre Libre, which will produce *Ghosts* in 1890.)

1882   *An Enemy of the People* (*En folkefiende*) published in Copenhagen. First performance: January 13, 1883, Oslo.

1884 *The Wild Duck* (*Vildanden*). First performance: January 9, 1885, Bergen.

1885 Ibsen returns to Munich, where he lives until
his return to Norway in 1891.

1886 *Rosmersholm*. First performance: January 17,
1887, Bergen.

1888 *The Lady from the Sea* (*Fruen fra havet*).
First performance: December 2, 1889, Oslo.

1889 April 15: The Freie Bühne is founded in a
Berlin cafe by a group of ten. As a private
organization, the Freie Bühne is not subject to
censorship. Its outstanding productions bring
about Ibsen's breakthrough and that of the
realistic theater, break the hold of French boule-
vard drama, and put the unoriginal playwrights
of the Berlin stage out of business. The Freie
Bühne opens on September 29, 1889, with
Ghosts.

1890 *Hedda Gabler*. First performance: January 31,
1889 at the Munich Hoftheater.

1891 Ibsen returns to Norway and settles in Oslo.

1892 *The Master Builder* (*Bygmester Solness*). First
performance: December 7, 1892, at the Hay-
market Theatre, London.

1894 *Little Eyolf* (*Lille Eyolf*). First performance:
December 3, 1894, London.

1896 *John Gabriel Borkman*. First performance:
December 14, 1896, London.

1898 All Scandinavia pays tribute to Ibsen on the
occasion of his seventieth birthday.

1899 *When We Dead Awaken* (*Når vi døde vågner*). First performance: January 26, 1900, Stuttgart.

1900 Spring: Ibsen suffers a stroke, which paralyzes his right side. In 1901 his condition deteriorates after a second stroke, and in 1902 he becomes bedridden.

1906 May 23: Ibsen dies in Oslo.

IBSEN'S DRAMATIC TECHNIQUE

Ibsen's main theme is self-emancipation
unattained because of the seeker's own deficiency. In
his realistic plays Ibsen was always in search of a
personality capable of precipitating a classic dramatic action. Clearly, drama was at a crucial turning
point. While Ibsen was not the first to depart from traditional drama, his rapid, brilliant breakthrough at
the Freie Bühne in Berlin, the Théâtre Libre in Paris,
and the Independent Theater in London established
him as the ancestor of modern drama.

Even so, it took him thirty years to conceive a
dramaturgy appropriate to his themes. Ibsen, who
came from what is intellectually a borderland prov-
ince of Europe and who had been relegated for a
time to the fringes of society, who had grown up in
an age of romanticizing heroic poetry and patriotic
Norwegian self-portraiture, began by taking Shakespeare, Schiller, Heiberg, Œhlenschlaeger, and Victor
Hugo as his masters and the expert, sophisticated
dramatic technique of Scribe and Dumas fils as his
models. In his first, prerealistic period, which ended
with *The Emperor and the Galilean*, he wrote chiefly

historical plays. Underlying even these early works is the basic theme of the discrepancy between strength and aspiration, between will and possibility, which Ibsen called the tragicomedy of the individual.

But various misapprehensions prevented the early Ibsen from becoming a master dramatist: his tendency to romanticism, his Nordic ties, his determination to write plays that would lay the foundation for a Norwegian national theater, and finally his interest in using historical themes.

Eugène Scribe's technique of intrigue and action-delaying developments is still superimposed on the plays and is exploited primarily as a means of effective presentation. Ibsen still subscribed to the traditional style of writing a play. Almost all of his protagonists are, in a wider sense, "pretenders." The difference is that in the late plays their striving toward greatness lies behind them in a past dimension, while in the early ones it expresses itself in outbursts of passionate action. The crisis of the protagonist endemic in Ibsen's work is at first hidden by noisy theatricality. In these early plays we sometimes feel as if we were in a hall of mirrors, where the characters of Ibsen's later realistic plays are coarsened into larger-than-life, hysterically distorted figures. Emotions are discharged in grandiose, high-flown language and converted into highly theatrical or melodramatic effects. (Ibsen's way of psychologically vivisecting his heroes and thus breaking them from within is remarkable.)

It is clear, too, that these characters, whose will keeps them in constant tension, are often motivated by hectic passions and violent fanaticism rather than moral independence in Schiller's sense. To be sure, we can already distinguish indications of the realistic theater to come (in Love's Comedy, for instance, or in The Young Men's League). Certainly a play such as *The Pretenders* earned its success through impressive dramatic competence. Nonetheless, so long as Ibsen presented his themes in romantic, heroic, or historical guise or limited himself to Norwegian problems, his own greatness eluded him and he remained old-fashioned and rather provincial.

Instead of spending time on a discussion of the early plays, which had no impact on world theater, I shall devote myself to close analyses of Ibsen's masterpieces. *Brand* (1866) and *Peer Gynt* (1867) cannot, however, be ignored, dominated as they are by two characters who appear again and again throughout the later plays behind new physiognomies. One (Brand) is a man who uncompromisingly postulates Kant's "formation of character and personality" and "unification of moral principle and way of life"; the other (Peer Gynt), a man who ruins his life by trying desperately "not to be himself," as Kierkegaard expressed it. *Brand* especially, a play which comes close to being a masterpiece, can stand as a sample of the prerealistic plays and their sometimes fanatically exaggerated pseudoheroism. Among the plays of the second period, *Peer Gynt* is important if only because here Ibsen hit upon a fifth-act solution that was to provide the structural prototype for his realistic plays. As he awaits death, Peer has to fight off materialized visions of unlived life and his late fears; these materializations, among other things, force him to review his whole failed life. This solution had decisive consequences for Ibsen: his modern theater was born when he began to conceive of the whole play as a last act. In his hands the traditional final act (usually involving death or transformation) becomes autonomous, and, as the prehistory is integrated into it, expands into a play.

What Ibsen was developing was a theater of the anti-hero. His characters do not transcend themselves;

at best, they overcome their immaturities. The function of the dramatic process is to emancipate them
from the past; from the nonpersonal and the prepersonal; from anachronisms of society, its moral
codes and doctrines; from atavistic ways of thinking
and acting. (The early plays are intended as biting
social criticism, but in the late works the failure of
the individual to achieve self-realization is divorced
from social factors.) While Ibsen skillfully shaped
this reliving of the past into an action reaching into
the future, namely, self-fulfillment, the inner form of
the plays derives not from man's being always ahead
of himself (as Emil Staiger, the distinguished Swiss
literary critic, analyzes it) but from his having lagged
behind himself. If the hero, as "a hoping, planning,
acting human being," anticipates his future existence
at all, he is usually occupied in creating a refuge of
life-sustaining lies. Thus, his dreamy or delusive anticipations often actually help him to evade future existence and make the regression permanent. The drama is
conceived as a recapitulation of the past; its objective
is achieved when the prehistory has produced its
effects. These effects are usually destructive, rarely
liberating, but they always bring everything out into
the open, at least for the audience.

The dramatic technique that Ibsen used—which
has long been labeled as that of "analytical drama"—
seems to derive from a classical tradition. But unless
the familiar comparisons of Ibsen's plays to Sophocles's *King Oedipus* are hedged with reservations,
they will lead to misunderstanding of Ibsen's work.
It makes little sense to examine a dramatic technique
without considering what it is devised to achieve.
According to the critic Siegfried Melchinger, Sophocles aimed at a denouement that does not destroy
the hero but allows him "a tragiheroic possibility of

human stature." Ibsen's aim is almost always an unmasking that will show that the hero has deprived
himself of the possibility of being human. Oedipus
takes wrong paths that are forced on him by fate.
Ibsen's characters, by contrast, drift about on bypaths,
into which their failure to take life seriously enough
has led them. The classical dramatist writes tragedy;
the modern one, tragicomedy. Lastly, in Sophocles's
play the audience, not the hero (who acts), is familiar with the prehistory; in Ibsen the hero usually knows
the prehistory (unless he has repressed it), while the
audience must be shown it in a skillful presentation.
This makes all the difference. Oedipus insists on the
truth; most of Ibsen's heroes try to avoid it. Sophocles, then, exposes the conflict between truth and
delusion; Ibsen, the conflict between truth and self-
deception. In Sophocles we identify with the hero; in
this case Oedipus, whom, as a symbol of the mythical
fate of man, we are horrified to recognize in this
dramatic context. In Ibsen, by contrast, the disillusionment of finding that the hero is not what he has
represented himself to be alienates us from him.

The challenge of making a résumé of the past into
a play and forcing his secretive characters into dialogue led Ibsen to develop a brilliant dramatic technique. We will try to show how ingeniously he solves
the problem in one play after another. The Berlin
theater critic Alfred Kerr described Ibsen's technique
as *erlauert* (capable of seizing the characters at the
crucial moment that illuminates), and the description is acceptable provided we realize that even in
stressing the artificiality it acknowledges the artistic
character of Ibsen's work. In fact, only Ibsen's tremendous talent for compression (which is really just
another name for artistic sense) made his plays possible at all. Everything hinged upon seizing what

Emil Staiger called "the pregnant moment," or what in the case of some of the plays might better be called the moment of crisis, when the present could be shown to bear the past within it or when it revealed the inner existential condition of the characters so inescapably that their prehistory could be presented.

This talent for compression is also forcefully demonstrated in Ibsen's ability to make everyday reality, which he seems to be merely presenting, serve his artistic purposes. To force a society bent on concealment to face the truth, he utilized reality in a remarkable way. This can be seen in his handling of characters, of stage properties, and other elements. No one makes an entrance without good reason; no scene is allowed to get out of hand; every character plays an essential part in the ultimate exposure; every detail is dictated by artistic sense. Although the minor characters are stylized into contrasting or background figures, they rarely degenerate into what Franz Blei calls "speaking tubes." They have their own logic, because they are the product of their own assumptions. According to Robert Musil, Ibsen is "a master at creating the features—one might almost say the deceptive features—of the human face."

The idiomatic directness of Ibsen's language has no artistic quality comparable to the form and meaningful force found, for instance, in the dialogue of Georg Büchner's characters, even when impeded by the use of dialect and by the intellectual dullness of the speakers. Ibsen's characters express themselves with an almost Spartan economy. Indirectly, though, his language can certainly be considered artistic. Every speech, no matter how incidental, carries implications. Behind the dry casualness of language and tone lies an unflagging artistic sense, an economy and energy that force the dialogue—sometimes even single words—to yield one

new revelation after another. Thus, the pervasive implications of the language always extend beyond the
immediate situation into what is to come and what has
gone before, knitting the whole play into a unity of
meaning.

As has often been noted, Ibsen's plays are interre-
lated in what Wolfgang Drews describes as "a pattern
of thesis and antithesis." This pattern can be seen in
the succession of *Brand* and *Peer Gynt*. Ibsen was trying to free man from any kind of fixation, no matter
what contradictory forms it may assume, such as life-
sustaining lies or rigorous doctrines, which make personal responsibility superfluous. Through dialectical
thinking he worked toward synthesis: he sought to
emancipate man from all ideologies that stand in the
way of his autonomy and to suggest a mediated self-
image, in which the self emerges into full consciousness, free of all limitations.

The antithetical *Brand* and *Peer Gynt* are followed
by the historical play *The Emperor and the Galilean*
which was intended to reconcile their polarity in what
Thomas Mann called "a higher uniformity." This play
presents the first sketch of Ibsen's "third empire,"
where every form of life has entered into a Hegelian
unity with its opposite. In *The Emperor and the Galilean*, Julian the Apostate is defeated in his attempt to
realize the utopian dream of a renewal of Christianity
through the primitive vigor of paganism. This is a
defeat for Ibsen too—at least for the "world-historical"
pretensions that led him to muddle his dramatic concept with bemused profundities and pseudohistorical
panoramas. The play was developed out of aspects of
areas of cultures and historical epochs; at the time this
was written Ibsen was still breaking down the com-
plexities of antithesis into the polarity of the western
and eastern hemispheres, the antagonism between

Christianity and paganism, the succession of one short-lived period of dominance following another. Not until his later plays does he control a dramatic method, which, within definite limits, focuses on apparently irreconcilable contradictions and presents them with telling effect.

Several critics have used Ibsen's utopianism to expose his limitations. Siegfried Melchinger, for instance, stresses the epochal significance of his work, saying that it initiates "the decline of the theater of illusion" and represents "the first step of antiillusion-ism." But he adds that the pioneers of truth and freedom whom Ibsen brought to the stage reveal themselves as "a gallery of illusionists," so that this antiillu-sionist crusade ends, after all, in illusion. These are certainly perceptive arguments against Ibsen's plays; because of that these arguments should be reexamined. Here I only suggest tentatively that in many plays Ibsen used utopianism as a dramatic vehicle; it replaces the "future existence" with which the characters must be linked—if only through their wishful, fantasizing anticipations—if they are to qualify as dramatic heroes at all. Whenever this ideology comes under discussion, Ibsen's language becomes sentimental and develops a tendency to pseudopoetic pompousness, though it may legitimately be asked whether this is not in fact Ibsen's way of divorcing himself from his illusionist charac-ters.

It may be useful to examine in which plays utopian-ism is presented as realizable. *Peer Gynt?* Certainly, thanks to a superimposed mysticism. *The Pillars of Society?* Probably, though at the price of a stylistic unevenness. *A Doll's House?* Possibly. *Little Eyolf?* Yes, though here the transformation of the characters is associated with such resignation and such a serious approach to reality that all illusionistic and ideological elements have been eliminated. All in all, in the plays of Ibsen's maturity, a fully realized transformation of character occurs only in *The Lady from the Sea*. It has also been largely overlooked that Ibsen often repudiated his heroes far more drastically than his critics do, often revealing their pretended vanguardism as atavism. For this reason, it is unjustified to hold such figures as Hedda Gabler, Hilda Wangel, Solness, and Borkman as evidence against him. Their illusionism is not his.

Certainly, Ibsen, whose vision of the future drew steadily closer to the ideal of humanity fostered by bourgeois society, did not look beyond bourgeois ideology but merely sought to free it from its distortions. In his "seriousness about moral man" (Heinrich Mann's expression) he remained faithful to bourgeois values as long as he lived. Yet this did not prevent skepticism from winning out and having the last word. In the epilogue to *The Lady from the Sea*, Ibsen, a son of "the rude nineteenth century," imbued with its "brutal, honest pessimism," as Thomas Mann described him, mercilessly exposed the vision of the "man of nobility" as what Nietzsche would have termed "a fictional fraud." This play reveals Ibsen's true complexion as Thomas Mann saw it: "an angry bourgeois-evil face."

PLAYS

Brand

Only in its theme does *Brand*, a "drama in
five acts," offer any hint of Ibsen's future significance
in world literature. Its dramatic technique, based on
superimposing several different conceptions, contrib-
uted little to the solutions that Ibsen worked out in
his major plays. The function of the plot is to provide
Brand, the pastor, with situations and a setting in
which he can come forward as a theologian after the
death of God. Brand, who subjects himself and everyone else to the rigorous imperative of "all or nothing,"
is one of the most provocative (and, hence, one of the
most naturally dramatic) figures Ibsen ever invented.

Yet Ibsen failed to confront Brand with an adversary
who is a match for his radicality and determination.
The opposition he encounters is fragmented among a
number of adversaries with dissenting opinions, none
of whom can ever attain Brand's stature, if only for
reasons of dramatic economy. In any case, one of their
major functions is to load the atmosphere with such
stifling narrow-mindedness that Brand will explode in
an eruption of absolutism. The conception of the drama
explains this inferiority in Brand's partners in dialogue.

Ibsen wants to contrast the man whose categorical will is to establish the unity and identity of his self with those who fear the radicality of a self that elects freedom of choice. The others therefore make only a half-hearted pretense of will, allowing themselves to be circumscribed by the restrictions of economic circumstances, convention, and laws. (In these characters, who, as Kierkegaard would have said, want desperately not to be themselves, Ibsen was ridiculing his fellow Norwegians.)

The cast Ibsen used in *Brand* is much more extensive and heterogeneous than that in his mature plays; the characters are also less—or not at all—individualized. Most of the characters are reduced to their professional functions or to archetypes (peasant and son, mother and child). Instead of introducing the whole cast on stage (or at least in the dialogue) in the first act, as he usually does in the later plays, Ibsen introduces additional characters right up to the fifth act, so that he is sometimes forced to set the action going again or shift its course or define attitudes that have not even been alluded to before. The talent for concentration and motivation, which later emerges so impressively, and his gift, later developed to the point of mastery, of inventing characters and situations capable of being exploited in many directions—these techniques show up only occasionally in this work.

The dialogue has not yet acquired its underground, cryptic, ambivalent quality. With a directness that is sometimes artistically shortsighted, Ibsen lets his characters declaim their opinions point-blank, even when it may be detrimental to them—although this kind of expression is actually only in keeping with the character of Brand himself. To get his characters talking, he does not hesitate to make frequent use of monologue or to let one person eavesdrop on others; sometimes he even

resorts to asides. The directness with which the characters express themselves increases the tendency to
sententiousness inherent in the rhymed verse.

Brand dominates the play forcefully; long passages
are devoted to demonstrating his superiority, individuality, and singularity. Yet he is by no means merely a
mouthpiece—exempt from Ibsen's usual artistic and
somewhat ironic objectivity—for the playwright's own
maxims and for his furious indictment of the Norwegians. Moreover, closer examination will show that
Brand's foundering is not due to the nature of his
adversaries who evade confronting their true selves.
The mere fact that his death occurs in the icy mountain
wilderness, far removed from the human sphere, while
struggling with God, indicates this. This is why Ibsen
could dare to cut Brand's antagonists down to size.

In fact, the play owes its stature to a dramatic con-
struction that uses the overt conflict only as a foundation. It is significant that even Brand's wife, Agnes,
whom he has converted to purity of will, finally repudiates his uncompromisingness, and this repudiation
foreshadows his ruin. Agnes acts according to the principle of love, which she has translated Brand's radical
ethics into; but far from winning her case, she cannot
even defend it against Brand's arguments. In the end,
she is shown incontrovertibly to have been right. Amid
the thunder of the avalanche that buries Brand, God's
voice issues from the heavens, proclaiming himself a
god of love. By this he makes Brand, this champion of
a concept of God endowed with all the old forbidding
primitivism and majestically aloof purity, a subject for
tragic mockery. We shall return to this point later.

Since the structure of the play depends upon the
character of Brand, the scenes are loosely assembled
and cover a period of several years instead of being
linked by a law of events that swiftly and inexorably

overtake the characters. Ibsen is not yet skilled at finding significance in everyday banalities; he often prefers to look for it in the major issues of life, in pathetically or sentimentally heightened situations, and especially in the moment of death.

In Act I, Brand is returning to his village as a "stranger" from the implacable glacial region which a peasant has refused to venture into even to visit his dying daughter. On the way down to the valley he meets a former schoolmate, Einar, and his bride-to-be, Agnes, singing and dancing their joyful way into a "life free from care." Brand turns away and goes on toward the village.

In Act II, Brand undertakes a death-defying crossing of the stormy fjord to aid a dying man with a heavy burden of guilt. Agnes, carried away by his unshakable determination, takes the helm of the boat when everyone else refuses. The villagers, debilitated by unemployment and starvation, ask the young minister to be their pastor. Agnes leaves Einar to marry Brand.

In Act III, which takes place three years later, Brand is living with Agnes and their child, Alf, in his rectory "at the foot of a steep mountain face." He refuses to bring the sacraments to his dying mother because she is still clutching the property she has acquired and clung to in a lifetime of avarice. Although his little son Alf is wasting away with fever, Brand refuses to leave the icy darkness of his fjord parish.

In Act IV, on Christmas Eve, Alf is dead. Brand mercilessly shakes Agnes out of her "idolatry" of the dead child, tears her away from her memories, forces her to give Alf's clothes, which she has treasured, to a beggar woman.

In Act V, a year and a half later, Agnes is dead, spiritually exhausted. In accordance with what he thought was her dying wish Brand erects a splendid, towering church. But out of disgust with the mayor, who wants to pervert the new building to serve a reformed faith, and with the dean, who hopes that the award of a decoration will bind Brand to a secularized Christianity whose only purpose is to embellish established ideology and morality, Brand plans to disrupt the consecration ceremony. Einar, "washed clean" after a dissolute life and now a missionary, reappears and declares that Agnes is damned. His self-righteousness strengthens Brand's determination. Brand exhorts the assembled congregation to forsake "ephemeral dust" and the "spirit of compromise" and ascend to the "realm of freedom's sunshine," the pure, icy world of the mountain heights. When the hardships and exertions of the climb become arduous and the life of their children is jeopardized, the villagers fall back, one after another. Only Gerd, a girl who roams about the mountains, remains at his side. Both of them are swept away by an avalanche.

The challenge of "all or nothing," on whose absolute validity Brand insists, is to put an end to life's restless drifting into arbitrariness and irrelevance in which the self dissipates itself. And the reward? Purity of will, the might of faith, the unity of spirit. Clearly, strict adherence to the principle of "all or nothing" would give the self identity and the capacity to commit itself by will and faith to the absolute. Brand believes (with Kierkegaard) that this act, through which the self steps into its own freedom and truth, originates in the "pathos" of will. For extreme intensity of the will presages an "inner infinity" and opens the halfhearted self to what Kierkegaard called "the binding power of the personality."

Perhaps it is these parallels that have led Ibsen interpreters to see in Brand's categorical demand Kierkegaard's "either/or," by which the self makes the leap from the aesthetic to the ethical state. But the comparison is misleading. It is true that in both cases the leap into the new reality succeeds through the act of choice—the decision—which makes man's freedom real. But the ultimate goal of this act of choice is different. According to Kierkegaard, recreated man recovers "the aesthetic in its relativity," that is, he recovers it under the law of ethics and personality, which frees the conditions of life from frivolous arbitrariness and pre-moral aesthetic spontaneity and firmly establishes it in the serious sphere of the moral. Thus, he succeeds in "gaining the whole world and using the world without misusing it."

This is far from being the case with Brand. He attains the irrevocability of his life's structure and the rigorous unity of self by negating all substance and strivings that are incompatible with his doctrinaire self. Indeed, he would rather negate his self than the "intensity of duty" that makes him unassailable. Therefore, his rigorous willing cannot integrate the self as a unity of multiple possibilities and decisions; it fences it in to make it unassailable. This is why the principle of "all or nothing" can be realized only through "sacrifice," and every sacrifice reveals its prototype—surrender of life. ("And even if you were to give everything but life itself, you must know that you have given nothing.")

It is therefore significant that when the villagers submit to Brand's will and let him lead them up to the deathly kingdom of the glacier, they become fanatics. Like men possessed, they close themselves to all argument, with the archetypal slogan of fanaticism: "Anyone who is not with us is against us." The absolutism to which Brand has committed himself cannot therefore be regarded as a mature form of the self. There is even something infantile about his unassailable will. He is quite oblivious of the conflict of values in which

one obligation clashes with another; he absolutely rejects compromise, which may represent a wise, humane
form of will.

Hence, Brand is incapable of bringing polarities
together in a synthesis. In God he sees only the Lord
who demands "heteronomous obedience," not the
Father who "deals justly through grace" (Paul Tillich's
expressions). He does not understand what the theologian Urs von Balthasar calls "the indirectness of
transcendence," the fact that the transcendent cannot
be attained except by mediation in the here and now.
For Brand, God has withdrawn into Old Testament
aloofness; Jesus Christ is a model to him only in his
self-sacrificing submission, not as a mediator who, as
Tillich said, makes the transcendentally divine accessible to man and hence concrete. Brand subjects everything human to a destructive heteronomy; refuses to
recognize the earth as man's home; has no pity for the
pain of hunger, poverty, and physical suffering; and
demands that people sacrifice their most intimate relationships.

Thus, unity eludes Brand on all sides. To protect his
will from all conflict and to make it irrevocable, he
raises one aspect of it to the level of the absolute. He
achieves his rigid sense of identity in the unchange-
able. His relation to God is determined by law, so that
instead of intuitively understanding divine will he
reifies it. His relations with other people are governed
by the empty dogma of "all or nothing" and by an
abstract justice, so that he fails to give them what they
need.

Since Brand mistrusts unity and synthesis and suspects them of being a compromise, he has no access to
love. This brings Agnes into focus again. When she
first comes on stage, she is committed to a love
divorced from reality and immune to fate, a love that

turns life and eternity into a dancing place for her own happiness. With a dreamy, playful directness, her nature, which in this state is dominated by unity and loving forgiveness, proclaims itself. The decision by which she opts for Brand does not change her nature, but it subjects it to ethical imperatives, thus helping it to mature. She no longer seeks a life "given to her to play with," but one that is willed by moral energy. Because this willing does not become independent, the willing self does not become the center of self, as it does in the case of Brand. It remains attached to love, which, of course, is equally directed toward the absolute and the supertemporal but calls for its attainment only as far as the concrete situation permits. This power of loving mediation is what Brand praises after her death: "In the tiniest things she could always see the flame of greatness . . . uniting earth with the dome of heaven, as foliage overroofs a tree trunk."

Since Brand judges and pronounces sentence in the name of heteronomy, his verdict on those who think differently deserves critical appraisal rather than mere acceptance. His mother is a nightmare of avarice— seemingly the very opposite of the rigorous spirit of· sacrifice that Brand himself displays. In a speech that seems to owe as much to the impact of cruel reality as to clear-sighted vision, Brand recalls how on an autumnal childhood evening he watched his mother greedily plundering his dead father's body. The roots of this greed, which drives her to amass property with an evil obsessiveness and cling to it with furious avarice, are only sketchily exposed. As a young girl, she was forced to give up a poor village boy and marry the decrepit but wealthy Brand senior, so that she was deprived of the trusting, world-opening power of love. Avarice is her way of deliberately nullifying the freedom to use both her spiritual and her material wealth without misusing it. Like Brand, she tries to preserve her identity (which binds her to the material, not the absolute) by raising one tendency of the self to the level of demonic absolutism. It is no accident that Brand exploits Agnes as mercilessly as his mother plundered her husband. This makes Brand and his mother similar. Perhaps it also reveals that his fanatically self-sacrificing "all or nothing" stems from the "no" to his mother, which has fixated him for life in a childhood trauma.

Einar, the convert to missionary work, is a mocking parody of the new man for whom Brand wants to prepare the way. He makes the New Testament idea of grace absolute and thus perverts it, going so far as to damn the unorthodox in the name of the principle that promises forgiveness. What God wants of man is the sin of corruption, so that his grace may take effect. Thus, the seriousness of will is carried to absurdity, and man is shown to be a creature who always wants evil and always does good. All the facts of life that leave their stamp on existence, not excluding birth and death, are "trivial"—an assertion that denounces the striving for absolute self-realization as a sin and as an arrogant work of self-redemption. Nothing but absolute immersion in God, willing acceptance of oneself as a child of God, can sanctify man. "How did [Agnes] meet death?" Einar asks Brand. When Einar learns that she met it with unshakable faith in the Lord God, he pronounces his verdict: "Only him? In that case she is damned."

Thus, Brand's mother and Einar both mirror Brand himself. They are offshoots of his primitive fanaticism, a fanaticism that makes his life grandiose. It is different with the dean and the mayor, in whom Ibsen is castigating spiritual and worldly representatives of dishonest halfheartedness. The dean does not take the Christian principle as a challenge to become a real self, to emancipate will, to relate to the superself. For him, Christianity is no more than a religious trimming for established order and bourgeois convention, useful for passing off apostasy from the self as orthodoxy and for stabilizing the existing system of unfree society by clothing it with the semblance of transcendence. He is bent on forcing man to wear "the uniform of the times" and to make self-development suspect as a sin against divine authority.

The mayor's customary attitude is conformity and opportunism. To quote Brecht, he is "concerned with survival." He places himself at the service of every majority, swears allegiance to every current of the Zeitgeist. To him, purity of will is simply political dilettantism. In his book self-emancipation is a danger to society and an obstacle to progress; at best, it is heroic romanticism, inebriated, vainglorious exaltation, an outdated ideology in times of starvation (an argument that, by the way, saves the mayor from being an out-and-out caricature). But to back up his antiindividualistic opportunism ideologically, he evokes the ideal of humanity (which Ibsen, like Thomas Mann, regarded as "the goal of mankind"): "Not to be one-sided—that is the lesson of humanity."

Gerd, the girl who inhabits the mountain heights, is a disturbingly enigmatic, disquieting figure, an outcast because she is believed to be afflicted with madness. Ibsen discloses her past only by gradual degrees. She is the daughter of the villager whom Brand's mother would have married if men respected the principle of love. When she rejected him, he turned, as though deliberately flaunting his individuality, to a gypsy woman in the service of paganism. Gerd is the fruit of their union. Her father is dead; her mother has disappeared after a dissolute life.

Brand's mother now develops into the menacing figure of an ancestor who has placed a curse upon future generations. The patterns of a tragedy of fate (which Ibsen was later to develop to the full in *Ghosts*) seem to be interwoven with the two other conceptions. Love points the way to the intelligible self. The idea that an offense against love can perpetuate itself like a hereditary curse is very characteristic of Ibsen. This recourse to the tragedy of fate is revealing because it adumbrates the "analytical drama," which makes man the ideologist of his bungled past. Of course, Ibsen had to transform these elements into a tragedy of the categorical imperative. In the case of Brand (and Gerd), he uses the compelling force of the past not so much to break the individual will as to reveal it. (And when their previously cramped, narrow wills are broken, they are liberated into the sovereignty of humanity.) Even in this play Ibsen obviously mistrusts the demands of the radical ethics that he is constantly tempted to make his own.

A dark anger casts the shadow of its wings over Gerd's life. While she cannot put a name to it, she visualizes this angry threat to her existence as a hawk, a nature demon that she feels is pursuing her. At the end of the play, when Brand, too, is pursued by the hawk, and when Agnes appears to him in a vision and urges him to accept life, he manages to conceptualize this demon. Its name is "compromise." In Gerd, as in Brand, a will that devastates the drives of life fights its way to dominance. Since her life originated in betrayal, she tries to strengthen her self (because she cannot achieve identity) into unyielding rigidity. She sings the praises of all that cools the instinctual drives: "There, avalanche and crag lull you to rest. The wind off the glacier preaches to you." Under the fluttering wings of anger she climbs up to the "ice church," a

crevasse in the glacier arched over by permanently frozen snow, where the hawk cannot follow her. As to
the fjord church, the Christian sanctuary, she pronounces the anathema: "It is too small." This statement
links her dialectically to Agnes, who will later use the
same words (misinterpreted by Brand as an urging to
enlarge the building architecturally): "The church is
too small." To Gerd, Brand's church seems to be built
to the scale of a compromise, which seeks to accommodate hardheadedness and halfheartedness. What
Agnes means is that it has no room for the sanctification of the earthly and of human conditions of life.

On several occasions Gerd identifies the hawk with
Brand, at first tacitly but later overtly—and always
when he is in danger of abandoning "all or nothing."
The stones she throws at the hawk fall on Brand as he
turns back to his village and crosses the fjord to aid a
man enmeshed in guilt. And as the rumor spreads
through the village that Brand is about to leave the
village to save Alf's life by bringing him to a healthier
climate, she sees the hawk flying away; "and the man
riding on its back . . . was the pastor." A vision appears
to her: from the sea and from graves emerges a heathen
tribe of troll-like creatures—parents with their children. But when Gerd curses Alf as an idol, Brand
rejects compromise and the vision is extinguished.

At the end the fates of Brand and Gerd strive toward
each other and merge. In a sermon demanding a break
with Christianity, which is "great . . . only in lying"
and which is forced to uphold an authoritarian society,
he raises his church to the stature of a "cathedral of
life." Now he goes to the roots of Christianity so ruthlessly as to destroy it. The frontier between the here
and now and the beyond is pushed to a point where
they coincide: with utter antihumanitarianism his claim
equates existence with essence. And so when Brand

is left alone in the glacial snow to fight off the final temptation—a vision of Agnes symbolizing the repressed impulses of his self—he is destroyed by the realization that his rigorous refusal to compromise has led him into the death zone of the "ice church."

Gerd joins him. With triumph she sees this "member of the ice church's congregation" staggering toward her. When she sees that he is bruised and bleeding, she sees him as a savior bearing the stigmata. And here she is right, for the "road paved with sacrifice," which he has trodden, the fact of being a man chosen by God and drinking the "sacrificial chalice" to the dregs, led to self-redemption. It was the desire to liberate his self from halfheartedness and untruthfulness, to make its will absolute and sanctify it, that had imprisoned the self in fanatical refusal to compromise. (This also accounts for Brand's desire to make himself independent of grace: "To beg for Christ's mediation, to stretch both hands toward heaven in supplication, while standing neck-deep in doubt—ah, if that were the solution to the problem!")

The realization that in climbing so high he has separated himself from God and man forces Brand to turn back. He acknowledges Christ, the mediator, accepts life and brotherhood (and this is the hidden meaning of his relationship to Gerd): "Born to a common doom, only in this way can our guilt be expiated." (In this play guilt is always a reminder that everyone is an inextricable link in the chain of generations.) Under the impact of Brand's reversal Gerd, too, opens herself to "the vast tent of heaven." The "glacier's shroud" dissolves, and her "mind thaws out in tears melted from the eternal ice." Now she kills the hawk, shooting it with a rifle she has stolen and loaded with "steel and silver." She watches it fall, its plumage gleaming white as a dove's—a fleeting sign that com-

promise is an earthly manifestation of love. Precipitated by the shots, the avalanche breaks loose, burying
them both.

Georg Brandes takes the closing words "God is love"
as a concession by Ibsen to the audience. This provokes
contradiction. In fact, love is a seeking not to deny the
seriousness of will but to save it from following the
wrong road of a self that overcomes its indecisiveness
in an orgy of radical self-sacrifice, and to point to its
goal. This goal is Kierkegaard's "development of the
personality," the self whose relation to itself should be
free, not fanatical, and whose relationship to God
should be human, not titanic. After God reveals himself, thereby confuting the uncompromising Brand,
Brand's ultimate fate hangs in the balance between
damnation and grace.

Peer Gynt

Peer Gynt is Ibsen's most self-indulgent play. In describing it as a "dramatic poem," he himself readily admitted its lyricism, its tendency to monologue and unrestrained flights of imagination. (It is not surprising that Grieg and Egk were inspired to set it to music.) Yet the exuberant language never overrides Ibsen's sense of form because it is organically linked with the title character, whose creative subjectivity is the mainspring of the play. Peer is the incorrigible rhapsodist and visionary, slick reasoner, liar, and dreamer.

Peer Gynt is largely unaffected by the realism of its day. It anticipates Strindberg; without doubt it had a stronger influence than any other play of Ibsen's on Strindberg, who despised him. In this drama the expressionists found a dramatic life ending in redemption, which fitted their goals perfectly. Ibsen expanded the extremely dramatic "two-soul system of Faust" long before Strindberg. "The Gyntian self . . . is a host of wishes, appetites, desires . . . a surge of moods, demands." The moods, longings, and fears that arise in Peer embody themselves in characters and cause

33

him plenty of trouble. He is therefore perpetually occupied with himself, so that the play loses its usual
function of presenting an objective conflict through the
clash of antagonists.

What Peer has to fight comes largely from within
himself. Many scenes are derived from dream and fantasy; sometimes we sense a monomaniacal element in
his monologues. W. Drews's good distinction between
Ibsen the "word-symbolist" and Strindberg the "scene-
symbolist" does not apply to Peer Gynt. The play is
ambiguous and lends itself to many different interpretations, at least in its details. Many passages are encased
in a cocoon of meanings. Since the nature of the play
precludes detailed commentary, I shall confine myself
to extricating the guiding thread from the tangled
skein of the plot.

Although Peer Gynt has five acts, it is really a three-
act play, presenting the three phases of the hero's life.
Acts I through III deal with Peer's youth, the transition
from adolescence to young manhood; Act IV, with his
adulthood; Act V, with his old age. (The inherently
epic character of the play is strengthened by the fact
that Ibsen did not shrink from annihilating stage
reality. This boldness makes the play appear highly
modern.) Apparently the leitmotif of the play is a symbolizing of the ages of man.

Peer, whom the Austrian theater critic Alfred Polgar
called "this rough sketch for a genius," has always been
regarded as the polar opposite of Brand. And indeed
the tests that separate the grain from the chaff produce
no permanent change in Peer, only outward ones. He
can dream, invent, and embroider; he can be swept
away; but will—any serious act of volition that calls
for translation into action—is beyond him. This is why
he has no real life story. His present is not rooted in
past experience, nor does it point to the future. He has

neither honesty nor steadfastness; word and experienced reality contradict each other. He never redeems
the promise of what he says and does. He refuses to
accept responsibility for the consequences of his
actions or for the obligations that await him. And how
should he, since his life does not spring from a will that
remains consistent through all vicissitudes of time? As
Kierkegaard said, "When we exclude choice, the personality unconsciously chooses, or the dark powers
within it choose for it."

Peer is an epigone; he belongs to a romantic era that
relives dreamily the age of heroes. He is hardly aware
of human and physical reality except in the form of
resistance and setbacks. He is in every respect pathetically uncontemporary. He cannot relate to his milieu
or his time—a world of peasants and artisans bound to
Christian conventions but only superficially civilized.
The unproductive Peer has no function in this society;
his fantasies transport him to a pagan, legendary
world. Last of all, he cannot even keep abreast of his
own life story. Instead of preparing him to take his
place in the adult world, his late adolescence is dominated by his mother, Aase. She is the only human being
to whom he returns.

The first three acts (which are considerably shorter
than the last two acts) take place in the hills and val-
leys of Peer's native Gudbrandsdal, in the early nineteenth century. His father is dead, having squandered
his riches in extravagant living. Aase's run-down farm
is about to be auctioned off. For years she has sought
escape from her misery, along with Peer, in fairy-tale
fantasies. The play opens with Aase's dramatic "Peer,
you're lying!" But by making himself the hero of a dar-
ing adventure story, Peer changes his mother's ironic
coldness into excited interest, thus gaining her sympathy—and that of the audience.

The scene quickly shifts to the wedding of Ingrid, daughter of a rich peasant, whom Peer might have married if he had not missed his chance. Peer, standing at the fence daydreaming, is induced by the girls to join in the festivities. He meets Solveig, destined to be involved with him in a lifetime of "celestial love" and thus secure his admission to the "host of the blessed." She is accompanied by her parents, newcomers to Peer's village. Solveig and Peer are spellbound by one another. Clearly, neither of them is an individual. Solveig, clinging to her mother's skirts, prayerbook in hand, "her eyes cast down toward her shoes," is "a child" (as well as a feeble copy of Faust's Gretchen). Peer is raggedly dressed, drunken and clumsy in his behavior, inert—an immature, conceited braggart. It should be understood that he and Solveig are foreign to one another; yet the loving glance of each senses the individuality of the other.

Ibsen now introduces a stark contrast to this encounter. The bridegroom, whom Ingrid has locked out of her bedroom, asks Peer for help. Peer is at the crossroads. Having no unity himself, he sees woman as two conflicting phenomena: the pure angel and the concubine. The dark forces within him make the choice. He forces his way into the bedroom and carries Ingrid off to the mountains. In acts like this—a rape of another man's bride, prompted by sudden desire, an imitative reenactment of the heroic age— Peer's nature expresses itself.

The second act finds Peer wandering through forests and mountain heights. After seducing the compliant Ingrid he has sent her away—incidentally in the name of Solveig, the mirror of his intelligible self. But the memory of Solveig does not hold him for long. He escapes from his pursuers by crossing the legendary frontier that separates the realms of the profane and the magical, breaking with society and Christianity. He has an erotic encounter with three cow girls screaming and shouting for "a troll to spend the night with." Then he succumbs to the lures of a woman dressed in green, daughter of the Troll King, master of trolls and kobolds. Before them a cave, the royal hall of the Troll King, opens on what is to be Peer's *Walpurgisnacht* on his roundabout way to redemption. There the king of the trolls is enthroned amid a horde of grotesque monsters. The empire Peer has always dreamed of will be his if he marries the king's daughter. He willingly renounces his entelechy, denying the imperative of the human desire to become ("be your-self") and accepting the first principle of trolldom: "Be sufficient to yourself." He acquires a tail and has already sunk below human level, but when he learns that his transformation into a troll will be irreversible, he begins to resist. Even to undertake to be a troll for the rest of his life requires more will than he can muster. The monsters fall upon him in a frenzy. He is saved only by a cry for help to his mother, whose image of him is more pure. Bells ring out as though proclaiming that man is indeed made in God's image.

Peer's next battle is against the Boyg, the twisted man, a shapeless creature of "mist and slime," whom Kurt Wais convincingly interprets as "the totality of all that has been," the past that obstructs the break-through to one's own self. Peer tries to slash his way "straight through," but the Boyg tells him to "go around." The Boyg refuses to stand and fight; the blows Peer strikes at the empty air only exhaust him, and he ends by scratching and biting himself in impotent rage. This time he is saved by an appeal to Solveig, who is mindful of his destiny.

At the end of Act II Peer sends a message to Solveig, telling her never to forget him. At the beginning of the third act he seems to have changed. The dreamer drives out the phantoms that fill his mind; the unproductive man sets to work; in the deep snow of the forest the aimless drifter begins to build himself a hut. Solveig's nearness grows into presence. Now that he seems worthy of her, she comes on skis to join him. Love has given her the courage to open her self, and Solveig has become aware of her individuality. Her actions now stem from freedom and finality. She has left her parents' home to follow the way she knows she "should and must take," the path of no return.

But Peer cannot master his "kobold thoughts." The troll princess appears, holding by the hand an ugly child born of their "thoughts and desires." A split personality himself, Peer cannot mediate between the "pure one" and the "nightmare." Telling Solveig to wait, he "goes around," runs away from the conflict to his mother, who alone has the power to free him from his personality. Having "turned away from his heavy burden," he reaches his mother's house, only to find her on her deathbed. In a scene of haunting brilliance the play now reaches its grandiose rhetorical climax. Peer talks Aase out of her readiness, inspired by fear of death, to face her own self-betrayal and end her life in despair. He lulls her with fantasies, and with his lies coaxingly talks her into believing the gates of heaven are open to her and that she will have eternal life.

Act IV takes place in North Africa in 1821, the year of the outbreak of the Greek war of independence. Peer is now in the prime of life. Ibsen has often been accused of stylistic inconsistency in this act, and it is true that there is a sudden change of tone. In the intervening years Peer has made his fortune in shady transactions and dishonest or downright crooked deals in America. Leaving the twilight of the past and the world of legend and paganism behind him, he has made the leap into the New World (as Borkman will do later), though naturally without shaking off the demon of atavism he has to contend with. He has therefore undergone no real development, although he has lost his naïveté. His lies and promises have, as it were, lost their innocence. His imagination no longer catches him off guard, tricking him into unreality. It now has a tinge of cleverness; he can set it going at will. His make-believe is no longer spontaneously invented on the spur of the moment but is carefully thought out.

Peer reasons and argues, offers specious proofs, calculates and calculates. There is something vulgar and affected about him. He copies himself. He has lost his old charm. Anyone who gets involved with him either has ulterior motives or is trying to take advantage of him. He presents himself in splended guise (as Crœsus, prophet and emperor) but is always made a fool of in the end because he acts imitatively rather than unconsciously; he plagiarizes himself. He has lost all that is most characteristic of him. Solveig does indeed reappear briefly, sitting outside the hut, transfigured by sunshine (a blonde counterpart to the Arab girl, Anitra, whom Peer is trying to seduce), but she appears only to the audience, not to Peer. Peer the adventurer has now made destiny his superself. He dismisses God with a wink as an accomplice or with a sigh as an amateurish bookkeeper of fate.

Peer's relation to tradition is disrupted, like his relation to his self, whose experience he records in a diary. The past no longer comes irresistibly alive in him; instead he has assumed the air of a man of the world and quotes from literary and popular sources, drawing egotistical conclusions from his quotations. His relationship to reality has also lost all its naïveté, and along with it its lively storybook quality. It is now detached, ironized, sometimes even caricatured.

The first scene of Act IV shows Peer, who seems to have matured into a sophisticated personality, entertaining a German, an Englishman, a Frenchman, and a Swede. This scene gives Ibsen an opportunity to satirize national characteristics. Peer's maxims no longer occur to him in flashes of dreamy, fanciful inspiration. He can now formulate them quite deliberately: "A man only needs to take care of himself and what is his." Eberkopf, the German, thoughtlessly retranslates this doctrine into Hegelian terms, so that Peer's way of life, ironically, turns into a Hegelian "being in and for itself." But the Hegelian concept of development is inappropriate: Peer is as out of step with his times as ever. In the Greek war of independence, which has aroused the enthusiasm of the progressives, he proposes, for the sake of the profits to be made, to support the heathen oppressors. Certainly, as one of his guests says, as a host he is heroic; but even in this pose he is merely imitating his father's extravagance. He still craves from others the esteem he cannot give himself. He has botched his manhood just as he botched his adolescence.

Peer's projects come to grief. His guests steal the yacht on which he has stored his whole fortune, leaving him marooned on the beach. (True, his prayers are answered, and the guests go up in smoke when the yacht explodes.) Now comes a series of scenes that once again reveal him as being out of step with the times. He spends the night in a tree, besieged by apes. The parallel between these monsters and the horde of kobolds in the Troll King's cave is pointed out. Peer shows himself as ready as ever to comply with weird, animalistic demands.

Then one of his childhood dreams is fulfilled: he acquires a "richly caparisoned horse," which escaping thieves have abandoned, along with the "sacred robe" of a desert chieftain. Dressed in the regal garment, he is hailed by a tribe of Arabs as a prophet. Peer becomes trivial and falls into a trite imitation of his own past. He seizes his chance to tame Anitra, the child of nature. Once again he has chosen a girl "without a soul." The play of false personalities becomes confusing. Peer knows that his prophet role is no more than another persona, and he assures himself that his true being, his true self, will come to light in a cooing tête-à-tête with Anitra. But the lover's role is just another mask, in worse taste than the first one, a sentimental repetition of adolescence. With affected vanity he reenacts his youth: "I'm young, Anitra!" Anitra easily enough gets the better of this self-forgetful character. After seducing her, he jumps up into the saddle behind her like a strutting cock. With a show of false tenderness she robs him and leaves him alone in the desert.

These scenes are as odious as stale plagiarisms. They are pervaded by faint echoes of Goethe's *West-Oestlicher Divan* and borrowings from the German romantic poet Friedrich Rückert (1788–1866), who was one of the first European poets to write adaptations of Oriental lyrics. All the standard props (palm trees and lute), mood-creating effects (moonlight), and symbols (nightingales) are there. The rhyme becomes richer and more mannered, in the style of Oriental poetry. Is this to be regarded as imitation on Ibsen's part? The obvious plagiarisms from Rückert are probably intended to characterize Peer in an ironic way. The style mirrors the anachronistic, secondhand quality of Peer's amorous raptures. This view is supported by Peer's expressing himself in deliberate parody and in a Heine-like disillusionment, which are clearly meant to be associated with the speaker and to suggest the dependence in which he lives.

Peer's fall into the "abyss of the past" cannot be stopped; his reflections become more and more remote. When his career as a prophet comes to a bad end, he becomes a tourist exploring world history. "He no longer wants to tread the paths of living men" but "to relive history, as in a dream." He begins in Egypt, which to Ibsen himself had seemed a "land of the dead." Then he comes upon the Memnon statue in Thebes. Apostrophizing Peer as an owl (which flies only when day, the time of productive perception, is waning) and invoking the symbol of the phoenix, the statue pronounces Goethe's law of *stirb und werde* (die and be reborn). Peer takes this for "the music of prehistory." The statue reminds him of the Troll King.

Next, he visits the sphinx who remains mute to his questions, and seems to resemble the Boyg, that is, the parts of the past that weigh upon him. When he asks "Who are you?" an echo repeats his question in Berlin dialect, and Begriffenfeldt (who has been made director of the Cairo insane asylum) appears from behind the sphinx. In sententious double-talk Peer tells him that the sphinx is a friend of his youth who "is himself." Begriffenfeldt believes that with this he is initiated into "the meaning of life" and enthusiastically drags Peer off to the madhouse. The Hegelian philosophy is rung out. Since "absolute reason" expired at midnight, the keepers are put in the cells and the madmen released. Egotistical affectation now turns into monomania, in which selfishness is literally carried to absurdity.

Three madmen are presented to Peer, "hermetically sealed inside the cell of self." There is no longer anything absolute that can be present in the individual. The *idea* has degenerated into *idées fixes*. The three madmen are obsessed by delusions that reduce them to puppets of the past or reify them. This is the very triumph of selfhood, for if madmen are to "be themselves," they must "be beside themselves." Their fixed idea precludes any freely willed thinking and radically blocks human and spiritual self-development that might be achieved by shaping their own world; yet they cling to it so resolutely that they are maniacally "themselves" in every life activity and remain hermetically closed off from the universal and absolute in which they might become spiritually free and open to the world. Goaded by their delusions, they literally cast off their humanity or vie with each other in trying to put an end to their lives before Peer's eyes. But the mad radicality with which they realize their selfhood is too much for Peer. Giddy from this enthronement of monomania, he tries to assure himself of the absolute, desperately seeks God's presence, but can think of no other name to address him by than "guardian of all madmen." He faints. Begriffenfeldt puts a straw crown on his head and proclaims him the Emperor of Self.

Act V takes place in the 1860s. The opening scene finds Peer, his hair now iron-gray, on board ship off the coast of Norway; later he will return to the Gudbrandsdal and the surrounding mountains. The return to his native soil strengthens and rejuvenates the Gyntian imagination, so that Peer regains the direct relation to reality that had previously been characteristic of him. His imagination calls up a multitude of figures, ranging from Solveig's bright, otherworldly form to nocturnal freaks. Having ridiculed Peer's adulthood as an imitation of adolescence, Ibsen now presents his old age as a mere repetition of his bungled existence, tending more and more toward the supernatural. Life drifts past Peer again. In a flood of encounters and "ghosts of conscience" (like those that have been observed in Strindberg) he seems to fall into nothingness. The fifth act anticipates Ibsen's late masterpieces in that it summarizes the botched past, a function that Ibsen later extended to the play as a whole. (The later plays are able to fulfill this function through subtle motivation and greater concentration of time and place.) The second half of Act V might be called a painful extension of the moment of death.

Indeed nothing but mask-destroying death could induce Peer to stop hiding his self under ever new "veils that serve to cloak non-living" (to use Goethe's phrase) and take a good look at his existence. His sense of approaching death now sets his imagination working. (The figures it creates are for the most part personified self-examinations.) It begins on the ship. As a storm breaks, an unknown passenger approaches Peer, gloating over the prospect of corpses. (This stranger, by the way, defies rational interpretation. He seems to speak from some offstage position, predicting a properly theatrical death for Peer when he has "seen the fifth act through." He also delights in the grotesque. To him, a joke is as good as "a solemn rhetorical style.") Peer is still concerned only with gaining a reprieve from death by eluding it in place and time; he has not yet faced its inexorability. (When the ship is sinking, he pushes the cook into the sea to save his own life.) But the unknown passenger has announced, "I'm waiting!" This establishes him as the counterpart of Solveig, whose steadfastness proves the time-defeating power of loyalty.

Peer's journey through his native country is marked by graves, rubble, and ashes. This backward journey through life is like casting off one husk after another—down to darkness, to use a phrase of Hofmannsthal—though in the end no kernel, nothing indestructible, is revealed. Peer finally radicalizes the experience of transitoriness and nothingness by comparing existence to a shooting star: "To flash, to be extinguished, and to vanish in a moment." The first stage is a leave-taking from those who have been involved in his life. Some of them have just died, but even to the others he does not survive as a living presence. (They say that he has been hanged.) His last possessions are being auctioned off. Peer himself puts his dreams and fantasies on the block. Then he finds himself all alone in a deserted forest. Rooting like an animal for food, he finds an onion, symbol of his existence: "What a lot of them— layer after layer! Will we never get to the heart?" This insight brings him for the first time close to Solveig. But confronted with her perfection, he is overcome by fear, by the stifling realization that his life has fallen irrevocably into nonexistence.

Night has fallen—the eve of Pentecost. Peer comes running over the moor. Now he is alone in the torture chamber of his conscience. All the unlived life, the unshed tears, the undone deeds crowd in upon him, calling him to account, threatening charges to be faced at the Last Judgment. From the depths of perdition Aase's voice joins in. Peer calls for a gravedigger to bury all these phantoms of his conscience, and the button-molder appears, casting ladle in hand. Peer, whose lack of steadfastness has prevented him from ever acquiring a personality, is to be melted down into matter and returned to the elements. When he promises to refute the charge, he is granted a reprieve until they meet again at the third crossroads. But no one will testify for him. The Troll King (by now so obsolete that he serves no purpose except in hopelessly anachronistic Norwegian drama) confirms that Peer is indeed an antiindividualistic troll. The devil spurns him because even his pursuit of evil lacked seriousness and firmness of purpose. Peer seems doomed to return "unspeakably naked . . . into nothingness, into the swirling mists."

But Ibsen still has in mind an epilogue in heaven. As earth renews itself in the dawning day, Peer experiences the Pentecostal miracle, the infusion of the Holy Spirit. The churchgoers' hymn in which spiritual life becomes manifest plunges him into terror, into the realization that he has divorced himself from his own destiny. He breaks into the lament that will be repeated by all Ibsen's heroes, sometimes frantically, sometimes with resignation: "I must recognize myself as dead long before my death!"

But Ibsen's cosmos is still wide enough to have room for powers of redemption, which can overcome history inherited and guiltily lived. Peer has again approached the sphere of Solveig. This time he struggles out of the button-molder's clutches and frees himself from the troll principle that bids him "go around." No longer does he seek to evade his purpose by submitting to the compulsion of the past. Now he goes "straight through," and this brings him to Solveig's feet, thanks to repentance, which enables man to reject the "constitution" of the self that is guiltily linked to the past and to cast his eyes upon the person who is the image of salvation.

So there is one other human being besides his mother to whom Peer returns. When we look more deeply, however, the distinction between them becomes blurred: the mother has long been merged with the wife. In turning to Solveig, Peer is really returning home. Solveig welcomes the repentant one as her "boy." Thus, old age, too, ends with a repetition of childhood, though this time it is not to be playfully relived as an imitation but morally pursued as a rebirth. Women had always stirred up the primordial in Peer: heroic gestures, deepest urges, pagan feelings, second adolescence—all pseudorenewals that enslave him to history. Solveig, however, releases the history-transcending element in him—"his destiny, as God's spirit intended him to be." She has kept his destiny intact in "her faith, her love, her hope," forces that are directed toward the intelligible. In returning to Solveig, Peer has returned to himself. Now he can be redeemed.

A Doll's House

Nora is in the long procession of dilettantes in life that winds through Ibsen's work. As György Lukács said, she is one of those figures "who are aware of their alienation from their own souls and seek to overcome it through a desperate determination to stand the test of events." This, then, is a play that must create itself as a drama as it goes along, awkwardly setting up the prerequisites for a dramatic action while the story (a recapitulation of the botched past) is unfolding.

Nora's marriage to Torvald Helmer, lawyer and father of her three children, has obstructed what Kierkegaard would call the genesis of her character. Helmer's aim in life, pursued with the tenacity of those who have an instinctive fear of the self and of truth, is to be "invulnerable." He therefore shuts himself up in his "masculine self-consciousness." He recognizes only traditional principles, backed by religion, morality, and law, that is, regulatory forces, which do not need to prove their value to man and to human experience but which shape them. The people Helmer admits to the inner circle of his life he treats as things, objects for his moods. One of these is Dr. Rank, whose suffering—for death has already beckoned him—creates, as Helmer says, "a cloudy background for the sunshine of our happiness." Another is Nora, his "sky-lark," his "helpless little thing." Helmer relegates Nora to a subhuman level, stylizes her into a seductive child of nature. He dresses her up, makes her perform a Neapolitan fishergirl's dance, then, when she leaves the stage, takes her back to his "lovely happy home," where she is still his "young bride." His erotic desires find their outlet in flirtatious seduction scenes, with their invitation to momentary pleasure. He avoids love because it would put an end to the stylization of his surroundings, which serves to gratify his clever egoism.

Like other egoists of Ibsen's whose life is empty, Helmer goes in for outward show and window dressing —for the charm that promises excitement. He uses Nora to be productive in an interesting way and to introduce a pretty, decorative element into his exist-ence. This has the added attraction of turning her into his own creation, for she radiates exactly the colors that most enhance his life. But those who do not lend themselves to what Hofmannsthal calls "his selfish com-binations," who presume to use the intimate form of address to which old friendship entitles them, or who are in any way his rivals, are banished from his sur-roundings. Naturally he justifies this on grounds of moral disapproval (as in the case of Krogstad).

It is true that Nora takes as much pleasure as the complacent Helmer could wish in playing the role of the charming little ingenue. Nora lacks all conscious-ness of self and does not aspire to any, because it might cost her her magic. The first word she utters is "Hide," and indeed, from the opening scene on, hid-ing, dissimulating, extravagant spending, and prevari-cating are the four cardinal points that set the limits of her life. She loves secrets. Through her self-concealment she indulges both herself and her husband. She consistently shies away from reflection and concentration on the self and from the seriousness that makes things irrevocable.

Reality in the sense of potentialities coming true is embarrassing to Nora. Any confession bothers her because it puts an end to the fluctuating interplay of being and appearance. How "unseemly" then that Rank, whose life has such an aura of death, should confess his love for her! As if he were not lovable precisely because their relationship has no future! For Nora is always trying to protect herself from the future, from self-realization. She hates worries because they force her to face the future. There is something troll-like about her, something that resists change, something that suggests the fairy-tale situation where utterance of the key word breaks the spell and transfers the bewitched one into a higher form of existence. But a child of nature playing hide-and-seek with the demands of a higher mode of existence is exactly what Nora would like to remain. On the condition that Helmer promises not to pry into her secret, her truth, she promises to "be an elf for him."

Of course, there are also social reasons for Nora's lack of freedom, and Ibsen reveals them. They stem from the patriarchal system of family and marriage. Even in her father's home, where she "was treated like a little doll," she knew only the kind of infatuation that complacently seeks its own reflection in the loved one, not real love, which seeks to liberate the partner to his or her genuine truth. She is aware that "from Papa's hands [she] passed straight into Helmer's." Since Nora has never parted from the nurse who took the place of her dead mother, the climate of her marriage is that of her nursery.

Because Ibsen has to dispense with characters who might force the dialogue into a dramatic action (based on the attainment of freedom), the drama is necessarily reduced to the genesis of character. Nora's past shows that her character belies her doll-like appearance. Eight years ago she defied her conventional and patriarchal orientation and revealed her self; yet rather than stand up for her self, she keeps it a secret. What happened was this: to save her husband from a possibly fatal illness, Nora borrowed money from Krogstad, a fellow student and long-time friend of Helmer's who now has a very dubious reputation; since Krogstad required a cosigner for the note, she forged the signature of her dying father.

"I did it out of love," says Nora in self-justification, as if recalling Saint Augustine's maxim: "Love, and then do what you wish to do." Only once in her whole marriage, then, has Nora had Helmer's uncorrupted nature in mind. To act in this way, she had to drop the role society had imposed on her, had to tear her will away from Helmer, whose selfishness had appropriated it as part of his own will, had to break the law. Here Ibsen has the makings of a play on the classical model. But in the social milieu he is attacking, there is no one who can cut the Gordian knot. This society has a moral code that prescribes many rules but does not tolerate moral fervor.

So Nora has completely returned to her puppet existence. To prevent her from putting the blame on her father, to compel her to accept the responsibility and force her self-confession, Ibsen uses the technique of the French drawing-room comedy—intrigue with plenty of tension-building delays. He handles the technique of the *pièce bien faite* (the well-made play) so skillfully that for the first time its artistic potentialities are fulfilled. Krogstad is the schemer: he blackmails

Nora by threatening to expose her forgery. He alone would have sufficed to force the development of Nora's character; but to integrate him into the play's artistic pattern and fit his scheming into its dialectical movement, Ibsen introduces another figure, Christine, friend of Nora's childhood and a past love of Krogstad's. These two characters, who meet again in Helmer's house after many years, are, as it were, grafted on to the play in order to get the action going. In addition, they serve as explanatory parallels and foils for the central characters.

Krogstad (who, like Nora, has also committed a forgery in the meantime) believed that Christine had rejected him, but the reality is that she accepted a marriage proposal from a rich man whom she did not love because of family pressure. They meet now as widow and widower, released from the misery of marriages that from the outset were in contradiction to the ideal goal of the common life of two people. Christine is troubled by the meaninglessness of her life now that she can no longer occupy her former roles, and Krogstad is a "moral cripple." As long as the audience accepts the central characters' masks as their true characters, these other two appear to be foils for Nora's happiness, which is immune to old age and the vicissitudes of fate, and for Helmer's unassailable moral integrity.

But suddenly, as Nora's past and character are pried into and laid bare, a new light is cast on everything. Through a shift of lighting (a technique which Ibsen uses ever more masterfully to unmask his characters), the positions are reversed. Against the background of Nora's disintegrating marriage, the marriage between Christine and Krogstad, which had previously failed to materialize, now comes into being. Now at last Ibsen's hands are free for the drama he is striving toward. Now he can get rid of the intriguer he needed to get the action going. Krogstad, who attains his ethos through Christine's love, is ready to ask that his letter exposing the forgery (which is already lying in Helmer's letter-box) be returned unread. Christine, however, dissuades him from this generous gesture. Helmer must see the letter, so that the way may be opened for the truth. A moral drive takes hold of the instrument of blackmail. Ibsen has freed his play from the' impropriety of using intrigue to precipitate the development of character. The real drama, leading up through dialogue to autonomous decisions, can now begin (in the third act!).

Having kept the truth hidden for eight years and two acts, Nora is also close to a resolution of this kind. The candles on the Christmas tree, against which the first act is played, have burned down. The costume ball is over. Helmer's words express naked desire. The concealing draperies fall. Nora is thrown back upon herself. Christine has left. Rank, victim of a perverted society, who is paying the price for his father's wild oats, has clearly announced his impending death. The dream events (which were linked with the vanished Christmas decorations and with the people who have departed) now recede, and the real events demand their consequences. Nora has danced her tarantella, the climax of the ball, with a realism that gives warning that she is about to break out of her role in an eruption of wild, freedom-obsessed passion. Rank has showed her the way by announcing with disconcerting coolness that "it's all up with him," thereby refusing to continue to lie to himself.

At last Nora finds the strength to say to Helmer, "Now you must read your letters." She is still, however, clinging to her last illusion—that he will make the sacrifice that will reestablish him as the hero she believed him to be when the play opened. Helmer is unmasked. Stripped of his invulnerability, he falls into a frenzy of anger and fear and denounces Nora. He lives in a topsy-turvy world. Since he interprets her in terms of his own egoism, Nora as the loving wife seems to him a criminal; he calls her sacrifice a "vile act." He makes it clear that marriage is for him an instrument of his own egoism: "The matter must be hushed up. . . . We must maintain the façade of marriage."

That very minute he receives the letter in which Krogstad puts an end to his blackmailing. He tries hastily to force Nora back into her doll-like role, to obliterate, as if it had been a dream, the only hour when they ever looked each other in the face. But Nora, now in everyday clothes, realizes that her willingness to let herself be dressed up is responsible for her real guilt. In full seriousness—and for good—she must now regain that refractory freedom to which she once, half playfully and heedless of the consequences, screwed up her courage. She breaks free of society.

But right after the almost programmatic declaration of women's rights in the closing scene, it becomes clear that Ibsen's hand has slipped: her break away from illusions shifts again into the illusional. Nora's road leads back to the beginning, to her "old home"; then it is lost to view. For in no case can her future life be like that of Christine and Krogstad. The dramaturgy alone precludes this; in a dialectical reversal from a play of intrigue into a drama of character, the choice they have made is no more than a transitional phase. They merely yield to necessity and accept the role and limitations within which they can be useful. They want "something to work for, someone to live for." They exchange the "duty to oneself" to which Nora is committed for duty to someone or something else. By allowing them to be "this or that," the role frees them from the necessity of being themselves. Nora, too, no longer wants to evade the finality of finding her destiny. But in her desire for full freedom she wants to emancipate herself from all mere roles. Breaking free into an infinity of possibilities, she seeks the reality in which her real self will become her destiny. Her new-found dramatic eloquence enables her to soar up into a higher form of existence.

Ghosts

In giving *Ghosts* the subtitle "a family drama," Ibsen departed from his usual practice of characterizing his works as plays. This indicates a reduction. Wishing to prevent his characters from being scattered among the multitude of social and professional activities, he assembles them more incisively than usual in a closed society. He wants to force diseases and processes of moral and spiritual degeneration —which would normally follow a chronic, latent course throughout a lifetime—to declare themselves and flare up into the acute stage. This malevolently crafty old magician, as Thomas Mann calls him, has picked his characters, whose physical and spiritual decay he wants to show, with such "sophisticated, diabolical artistry," and has placed them in such a hellishly constricted situation that character after character is forced to interrogate and expose another.

Five people are subjected to this treatment: Helene Alving, widow of Captain (and Court Chamberlain) Alving; her son, Oswald; Regina Engstrand, Alving's illegitimate daughter; Engstrand, the carpenter, who is Regina's foster father; and Pastor Manders, Helene

Alving's girlhood lover. Mrs. Alving and Engstrand have kept Regina's illegitimacy a dark secret, just as she and Manders have concealed their episodic love affair. All these characters owe each other so much gratitude and recognition, so much support and assent (extending even to unacknowledged kinships and missed chances of marriage) that many of the words they exchange—sometimes even the very forms of address—inevitably turn into lies simply because they conceal or ignore the other person's individuality, identity, and origin. To force them to expose and return to the self, Ibsen has cornered them in a situation in which the self is inexorably brought to trial and convicted of bungling its past.

The unity of place is observed; the three acts all take place in the same room, with a view into the garden, with a drizzling rain outside. The plot is condensed into a unified action. The time, extending from one morning to the next, is limited to twenty-four hours. The forceful thrust of the three acts, into which the time span is articulated toward the poignant closing scenes, contributes greatly to the impressive unity of the play. All three acts lead up to a moment of truth, a recognition scene or, characteristically, in the case of Acts I and III, a recognition of the past in the present. Thus, each act reflects in miniature the inner form of the play, whose basic purpose is to get at the truth. (This explains why the dialogue keeps falling into the pattern of an interrogation and confession, a denial of the indictment and a defense.) This recurring pattern makes inescapable the dramatic events, which develop as the truth comes to light.

Time is measurable, measurable even by the movement of the stars, for the play spans the period from one morning to the next. Nevertheless, this progression does not imitate the irreversible sequence of objective time. In this case, time is the mode in which truth, as yet concealed, appears (just as the dawning of the new day is meant to be not only an astronomical event but also a process of unveiling as the truth "comes to light"). The truth dates back beyond the present in which the events of the play take place, although the dramatic action is set in motion because this truth is wholly or partly unknown to the characters and now comes to confront them. Strictly, then, the truth does not advance: it suddenly appears, and the present is then seen in the consuming light of the past. Time distinctions become meaningless; past events become actual; the past recurs in the present, and the present even reverses itself into the past. Truth is nothing but the mind-shattering discovery that time as a chronological process and time as a medium of moral and spiritual progress conflict with and annul one another.

Recurrence, return, and reversal are the fundamental configurations of this play. We should not forget that the Norwegian title *Gengangere* literally means "returners." Indeed the dramatic action is made concise by being basically conceived as a return—a return of the morning. The most pernicious form of return that occurs in *Ghosts* is the reestablishment of the premoral and the prespiritual, for the process of events leads to the destruction of the family, the moral and spiritual cell from which the organism of society develops.

This regression to barbarism originates in Ibsen's own version of the Fall—the reification of man. It begins to undermine social relationships when a human being is esteemed no longer for his own sake but only for the goals and purposes he can be made to serve. Ultimately, his value can then be expressed in terms of money: he degenerates into something that can be bought and sold. And indeed a symptom of the wrongheadedness afflicting the characters in this play is that they all, without exception, have their price.

The chain of causality begins with Helene Alving. As a young girl, instead of marrying Pastor Manders, whom she loves unselfishly, she sells herself to Lieutenant Alving "for the sum of his fortune." There is, to be sure, some excuse for her surrender of selfhood. After the early death of her father she was brought up by her mother and two unmarried aunts, receiving an early training in reification. As Ibsen demonstrated in such later plays at *The Wild Duck* and *Hedda Gabler*, in which the two-aunt constellation recurs, unmarried women and widows are more likely to degrade their charges by making them objects of their wishes to arrange other people's lives than to educate them to the freedom of responsible adulthood. People like this force girls into the marriage market.

Helene becomes the property of Lieutenant Alving. This self-surrender produces an almost automatic series of causal effects that annul human autonomy. Since at the time of his marriage the Lieutenant is bent on the pleasures of life like a child, he is not a person to Helene and cannot bring about in himself or Helene moral growth either in thought or behavior. Since he never found a role or the kind of people to engage him completely, he cannot accept himself. His desire for emancipation turns back upon itself. Because the forms of society deny him self-realization, he seeks an outlet in escapades and tries to attain it through a moral atavism, which Ibsen has described as Viking-like or troll-like.

During this phase of her marriage Helene runs away to Manders. But Manders shrinks from the act of freedom (the only one in the whole play) that restores man to his proper place in a social order. Helene returns to Alving. It becomes increasingly clear that the power of the past bends the fate of the individual characters, forcing them into regression. A traditional formal code of duty plays a significant part in this backsliding of the personality. Both Helene and Manders invoke duty or sense of duty whenever they need to motivate or justify modes of behavior incompatible with an innate sense of values.

This ethics of duty, which drives Helene back to her morally bankrupt marriage with Alving, fits exactly the social order that treats human beings as replaceable and interchangeable. It produces an attitude of will that loses sight of the individual. It prevents man from relating to his own self and to other people. Since it makes its demands in the name of a traditional principle rather than in view of actual human beings, it does not individualize action, does not ground action in moral knowledge, and does not let action be determined by ethical value. Helene's relation to Alving is proof of this. She accepts a principle (of marital fidelity, for instance) that makes her seem good but does not accept Alving as having the quality of goodness. Alving becomes merely an opportunity that enables her to be good.

Even the birth of their son Oswald does not save the Alvings' marriage. Alving is already afflicted with a latent syphilis, to which he will succumb after a lingering illness. Oswald has inherited this disease, which causes degeneration and disintegration of the personality, although it does not show itself until he is on the brink of manhood. In this case, since the individual has no freedom of choice, the causal mechanism rules supreme. It is therefore debatable whether Ibsen can use Oswald for a valid demonstration of social man's tendency to backslide. By making Oswald the victim of a congenital disease Ibsen left this drama as something between a period piece and a timeless tragedy.

As Alving's morality increasingly disintegrates, his social status grows. He gets his captaincy and is given a high-ranking court position. The esteem he enjoys is due to his acquisition of real estate, for which he received "all the praise—all the credit." Yet his success is not the result of his own virtues and diligence; he is far too degenerate for that. It is entirely due to the efforts of his wife. Of course, she has at heart not Alving's interests but those of her son, for whom she wishes to preserve a refuge, a "home." Appearance and being are splitting apart on all sides.

When Alving starts an affair with the housemaid Johanna and she becomes pregnant, Helene sends the seven-year-old Oswald away. But she does not do this to help him to "make a fresh start" (compare with *Hedda Gabler*). Helene stakes her existence on a life-long attempt to hide the truth (Alving's disintegrating personality) from her son and from the rest of the world. By preventing the unmasking of Alving, she makes it impossible for Oswald to divorce himself from his heritage and establish an autonomous life. She sends him away only to make it more certain that he will come back to her. (That Oswald is already incurably afflicted by syphilis is an undeniable stumbling block to Ibsen in his social criticism.)

Helene does not help Oswald to transcend his father. She fails to open his eyes to society's development-arresting laws. She wants to keep him dependent on her. Ibsen calls attention to this propensity for regression by revealing matriarchal tendencies in Helene that were conspicuous in the nineteenth century. She "assumed full control of the household," saw to it that "Oswald . . . did not inherit a penny from his father," tried to make it seem as though her dead husband "had never lived in this house." "There will be no one here but my son and his mother," she says.

Her method of winning Oswald back is revealing. With the idea of founding a charitable institution, she has put aside money every year since her husband's death until she has accumulated "the exact sum of the fortune that once made people consider Lieutenant Alving a good match." To assert her claim to ownership of another human being, Helene does not atone her guilt but pays off her debts. She tries to buy Oswald back. The name and purpose of the charitable institution are equally revealing. It is to be called the Captain Alving Fund and will support a children's home. Once again names and titles are clearly shown to be transferable, since they do not belong to the individual. Nor is the act of charity performed for the sake of its ostensible beneficiaries. The tragic connection between Helene's determination to build a home for children and the situation of her own son becomes clear by the end of the play.

Johanna, the housemaid, whom Alvin has gotten pregnant, is sold off to Engstrand, the carpenter, for a dowry of three hundred taler—another commerical marriage, upon which Manders unsuspectingly pronounces the blessing of the church. When Johanna dies, Mrs. Alving takes Regina, the daughter of Johanna and Alving, into her home as a maid. Regina's life, too, is subject to the power of the past.

So much for the prehistory. The action takes place on the day before the dedication of the children's home, which will set the seal on the lie. A dialogue between Helene and Manders, consisting of accusation, defense, counteraccusation, and self-censure, recreates the past. Manders, who has not seen Helene since their joint renunciation of freedom, has been named trustee of the institution and comes to see her on business. His early training in the renunciation of emancipation, which goes under the name of self-conquest, has prevented him from developing "the spirit of wilfulness." He is "the same as he always was —an overgrown child," except that he is now "up to the eyes in committee work." His urge for self-development has been stunted through "considera-ations" of various kinds; his actions are oriented to the views of "those who are entitled to opinions," that is, to an establishment ideology disguised as morality. Helene is happy to have Oswald home again; he has returned from Paris, where he has been a painter, to attend the opening. Engstrand, who has done the car-pentry in the new building, is also introduced.

Only when the prognosis of "incurable" has been pronounced does Ibsen take up the dissecting knife. He initiates no cure but confines himself to showing how the tumor originated and developed. In the dia-logue the prehistory breaks into the present, obscuring it and reversing it into the past. The theme of the play is, in fact, return—of the past. This theme expresses itself with rigorous unity in the structure of the play and dictates every detail of its formal principles. Time stands still as in the graphic representation of the cycle of astronomical day.

By constantly relating the present to the past, Ibsen reveals the enigmatic nature of time. This procedure, which strives for dialogically presented revelation rather than resolution reached through dialogue, has rightly been criticized as undramatic, although we have to admire the way it hangs together artistically. Of course, the characters do not discuss the past for three acts; rather, the truth comes to represent an event, becomes their destiny. Ibsen also makes master-ful use of his treatment of time in delineating char-acters and unmasking them indirectly. He uses it to reveal the end in what appears to be the beginning and to expose what seems to be individuality as an unproductive variation. This method, which makes the present susceptible to the charge of anachronism, is used particularly effectively, together with the technique of contrasting and parallel situations, in the case of Oswald.

Oswald is linked with his father by words and behavior so often, and sometimes so poignantly, that from his first appearance on stage he acts like a personification of Alving rather than like a person in his own right. The father returns in Oswald. In the first act Ibsen has so skillfully blended and interwoven Oswald's entrances and the dialogue between Helene and Manders (which exposes the truth about Alving) that the son points backward toward the father and the father forward toward the son. Thus, every forward-looking word that Oswald speaks is refuted the moment he utters it. Tiredness insinuates itself into his most animated gestures.

This associative technique reaches its climax at the end of Act I, when, within a brief interval—almost synchronistically—a sentence is repeated word for word. Helene's repetition of Johanna's cry of "Let me go!" as she fought off Alving is echoed by Regina's voice from the adjoining room gasping the same words as she repulses Oswald. At the very moment when Helene believes she has delivered herself from the past and can look forward to a fresh start, the present is transformed into the past.

Oswald, like his father, yearns for "the beautiful, splendid life of freedom" and "the joy of living." But this desire for "sheer joy in being alive" takes shape only in his painting: his favorite subject is man liberated to his utopia. Oswald is also forced to retrace his father's footsteps in his relationship to Regina, whom he believes to be the housemaid. In this "splendid, lovely, wholesome girl" he finds what is missing in himself, something to compensate for his lack of being, whereas Regina sees her relation to Oswald merely as a chance to "make the most of her youth" and become a person of consequence.

When Oswald's illness becomes visible and Regina sees that what is required of her is a relationship based on selflessness rather than self-advantage, she finds a more profitable way in which to utilize her youth. And as Oswald's disease progresses, another component in his relationship to Regina comes to the fore. He senses and searches for a sisterly element in her, hopes for the helpfulness and spirit of sacrifice that will finally give her the strength to perform love's most paradoxical service. It is certainly significant that Oswald's turning to Regina has an incestuous element, although he is quite unconscious of it. This is significant not only because such a turn would represent a return to an archaic form of marriage but also because even romantic love, which usually drives people away from home and family, ties Oswald to his family. This is why in the end Regina's place can be taken by his mother. Oswald's relations with women is of no help to him in casting off the spell of the past.

In Act I the final preparations are being made for the dedication of the children's home. Act II finds Engstrand engaged in a parallel—and contrasting— activity, which has already been hinted at in the first scene. He is planning to open a "home for seamen" as a front for a brothel, and he craftily tries to flatter Regina into coming to work for him. The inspiration that suggested this contrasting motif to Ibsen is diabolical in its grandeur and consistency. This parallel is also important because in the one case a father is trying to gain control of his daughter; in the other a mother, of her son. Since the audience is challenged to compare the two, the Engstrand-Regina relationship constantly casts a gloomy light on the Helene-Oswald one. The audience becomes aware of the immoral element in the mother-son relationship.

Engstrand is a cripple; a violent altercation with some sailors has left him with a limp that hampers his natural dynamism. He is also a schemer who would be a credit to Schiller, who created memorable connivers. He maintains shady connections with the underworld of the waterfront, to which he would like to return. Not only in *Ghosts* but also in plays such as *The Lady from the Sea*, Ibsen depicts this milieu as presocial because of the seafarer's unchecked tendency to roam far and free and also because of the interchangeability of human relationships, which depend upon accidents of place and opportunity.

While the other figures are the victims of social conditions, Engstrand, the only character in this play who does not have to confront the truth, is the person who destroys the others morally. His life, like those of the other characters, is based on lies. The actions of the others turn into self-betrayal because they hide their endeavors behind a façade of duties and moral pretexts (which, of course, inevitably leads to their deceiving other people). Engstrand, by contrast, deliberately and methodically sets out to deceive them. (Helene, it is true, is drawn with firmer, cooler strokes than Alving and Manders.)

The others act against their selves, set themselves in opposition to their own development. Engstrand knows how to steer everything to his own advantage through a systematic, calculated repudiation of morality. In him evil is unflawed and absolute. Ibsen did not find it necessary to explain his actions by past involvements, although his physical disability is obviously a clue. For this reason we do not feel the same benign concern for him as for the other charac-

ters, in whom we see the foundering of potentialities
for modes of life and living compatible with human
dignity. This is particularly true of Helene, who develops a self-searching—and, toward the end, even a self-
accusing—tendency, and of Oswald, who has the
capacity for a free spiritual relationship to the world.
And it is also true of Manders, who seems cut out for
goodness and conciliation. Engstrand, by contrast, is
not really in conflict with himself but pretends to be in
order to create the impression of a struggle between
his ego and his self.

So far as worth or worthlessness is concerned, the
play leaves Engstrand's fate undecided. Because he
resists morality, which stands in the way of man's
autonomy, he is the only one who achieves emancipation. In him the tendencies to reification inherent in
society attain self-consciousness, and with it extremism
and consequence. He draws final conclusions from the
premise that the social order rests on the fact that indi-
viduals are exchangeable. He embraces depravity but
disguises it with a masterly display of sanctimonious-
ness. Concealing his unscrupulous egoism behind a
posture of altruism, he manages to make the action
through which he drives Regina and Manders into
moral bankruptcy for the sake of his own advantage
look like benevolence. He misrepresents the brothel he
is planning to open as a "home" for seamen. His masterly use of methods of this kind is demonstrated by
the fire he sets in the Captain Alving Home for Children. He shifts the blame for this onto Manders, only
to take it back again—for a price. His words, "I know
of one who's taken other people's guilt upon himself,"
are a monstrous blasphemy as he talks of his sordid
bargain in terms of the most sublimely spiritual
exchange the world has ever known—the vicarious
atonement of Jesus.

At the end of Act II the children's home, the memorial to Alving that was to preserve his reputation for posterity, goes up in flames. The third act is the most brutal epilogue to bourgeois culture Ibsen ever attempted. First, Manders succumbs to the temptation of paying bribery. He buys himself free of his imagined guilt by turning over the income that will still accrue to him from the Captain Alving Fund to Engstrand for his seamen's brothel. This establishment will be named The Chancellor Alving Home, thus replacing the burned-down children's home. And indeed the two have undeniable features in common.

In exchange for her place in the children's home, Regina will now go to work in Engstrand's establishment. Just as Mrs. Alving was going to buy Oswald with the price of the home, Regina will be put up for hire by her father in the brothel. Thus, the second home is in a real sense the successor of the first. The only difference is that everything has become cruder and more outspoken. This intensification emerges again in the way Helene's undisclosed self-surrender to Manders is sharpened into Regina's open prostitution. This is another sardonic reminder by Ibsen of the causal nexus, as is the fact that Engstrand's establishment will profit indirectly from the price Alving paid long ago for Helene. The conclusion Ibsen wants us to draw is forced upon us: the organized immorality of the brothel—the only project in this play that has any future—is the extreme expression of a social order that prostitutes human beings. Love occurs only in the degenerate form of a purchasable commodity.

Oswald's return to his mother, as we have already showed, is the counterpart of Regina's return to her father. While the father-daughter relationship is commercialized, the mother-son relation reverts to an instinctual tie, reduced to the need for food and nur-

Alexander Moissi as the doomed OSWALD in Max
Reinhart's 1906 production of *Ghosts* at the Kammer-
spiele, Berlin.

A touching farewell between Ruth Gordon (NORA) and Paul Lukas (DR. RANK) in the New York revival of *A Doll's House* of 1937.

Tore Segelcke as an intense HILDA and August Odd-
var as a perplexed SOLNESS in a 1939 production of
The Master Builder at the National Theater, Oslo.
ROYAL NORWEGIAN EMBASSY INFORMATION SERVICE

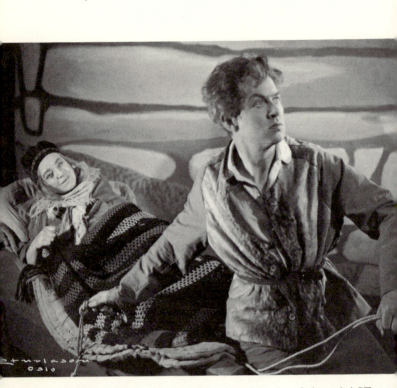

PEER (Hans Jacob Nilsen) with the dying AASE (Ragnhild Hald) in the Norske Teatret's 1948 staging of *Peer Gynt* in Oslo.

ROYAL NORWEGIAN EMBASSY INFORMATION SERVICE

A scene from Arthur Miller's version of *An Enemy of the People* (New York, 1950), with Florence Eldridge as MRS. STOCKMANN, Art Smith as her father, and Frederic March as DR. STOCKMANN.
CULVER PICTURES, INC.

BRAND (Per Sunderland) preaching to the gathered
townspeople in a 1953 production of *Brand* at the
Folketeatret, Oslo.

The unhappy Ekdalls—HJALMAR (Werner Hinz) and GINA (Ehmi Bessel)—futilely trying to converse, in Rudolf Noelte's 1956 staging of *The Wild Duck* at the Deutsches Schauspielhaus, Hamburg.

ROSEMARIE CLAUSEN

75

Claire Bloom as the sad, mature NORA, rejecting the efforts of her husband TORVALD (Donald Madden) at reconciliation, in the 1971 production of *A Doll's House* in New York.

ture in the one and the mothering instinct in the other.
A "terrible fear" announces that Oswald's disease is
about to enter the paralytic stage, a fear whose dark
threat imperils his individuality. Oswald's paralysis
demonstrates disintegration of personality as starkly as
Regina's prostitution. Helene, whose whole life has
been devoted to maneuvering Oswald back into the
nursery, is grimly taken at her word. Her son is
restored to her—infantile for the rest of his life. She
herself is finally fixed in her maternal role. There is
even the possibility that she will agree to "lend him a
helping hand" and take back the life she gave. This
would be a second form of degenerate love, one that
negates human beings.

Before the curtain falls, the sunrise can be seen
through the windows of the room overlooking the garden, arousing in Oswald an instinctive, childish
demand for "sheer joy." The circle has closed.

An Enemy of the People

At first sight Dr. Thomas Stockmann looks
like a classical hero, who positively invites us to identify with him. Yet this is not borne out as the action
unfolds. Even before he makes his first entrance, his
laughter and shouting tell the audience that he is an
impetuous man, and in the course of the action he
grows more and more uninhibited and uncontrolled.
Stockmann is obstinately rooted in his own nature, thus
he is not likely to founder in catastrophic situations.
This casts an ironic light on him. When Ibsen suggested that Stockmann, the unswerving champion of
truth and justice, is also a "grotesque" and "muddle-
headed" fellow, he must have had in mind Stockmann's
tendency to turn catastrophe into comic situations
(which makes one indestructible) and also his inability to become aware of his impetuous nature as it
clashes with the circumstances it encounters.

In the first act Ibsen prepares the way, through the
exposition of character, for the passionate battle over
truth that Stockmann will later precipitate. Stockmann
is a vivid figure, striving for fullness of life; his very
extravagance is attractive. The minute he comes on

stage, he casually lets us know that he enjoys good food. He makes no bones about anything, carelessly repeating his wife's words: "Katrine says I'm earning almost as much as we spend." Clearly, he is a man who lives beyond his means, a man with a tendency to excess and extravagance. This comes out even in his way of speaking; he is given to "rather strong expressions." Free and easy communication is his line; his natural way of asserting himself is to invite everyone to his home.

When the play opens, Hovstad and Billing, editor and assistant editor of the liberal *People's Messenger*, are enjoying an ample and delicious meal as they wait for him at his house. When Stockmann finally returns from his walk and joins his guests, his characteristic charm and directness are immediately demonstrated: he brings with him another, unexpected, guest, Captain Horster, whom he has run into on the street and persuaded, after some initial resistance, to come along. (Ibsen is, by the way, also eager to get Horster on stage, because if it were not for him the action would bog down after the third act. With admirable economy of means, Ibsen introduces in the first act a figure he is going to need in the fourth.)

Stockmann has something of the pioneer about him; there is something of the self-made man in his spontaneity and indifference to rank and position. The story of his life illustrates these qualities. Born of a poor family in "a dreadful little hole up in the north," he has worked his way up in the world and now lives with his wife, his sons Ejlif and Morten, and his daughter, Petra, a teacher, in a town on the south coast of Norway, where his brother Peter is mayor and holds several other official positions. Soon after Stockmann arrived in the town his "ideas"—never in short supply —bring it new prosperity. His discovery of medicinal springs turns the little town into a spa enjoying an annual bathing season.

Stockmann revels in a joyous sense of beginning, which anticipates Brecht's Galileo: "I feel so indescribably lucky to be a part of all this fertile, germinating life. Aren't these splendid times to live in? It's as if a whole new world were springing up around us." His exuberant vitality drives him on; the vital sap must keep flowing. He senses "great promise . . . so many things worth working and fighting for—and that's what's important." He has an urge to "stir up the fermenting stuff of the future." And he rubs his hands. As Nietzsche said, speaking of sex, the "degree. and mode" of his vitality "reach up to his highest peaks of spirituality." Everything he embarks upon stems from his boundless lust for life.

This is the audience's impression of Stockmann when the moment arrives, at the end of the first act, that will make him the protagonist of the play. He receives a letter confirming a suspicion he has long harbored but kept to himself: a chemical analysis by a university of the town's drinking water and the water supply of the baths proves that the feed-pipes leading to the pump house are contaminated with dangerous bacilli. And the bathing season is about to begin.

Stockmann's reaction to this catastrophic news is instructive. "Flourishing the letter," he enters the room where his family and guests are assembled and announces "some news—a great discovery." He seems pleased and excited that the prevailing belief about the healthfulness of the little town has been exploded, and he uses "strong expressions" to bring home to his listeners how the situation has changed: "The whole spa is nothing but a pesthole, a whited, poisonous sepulcher." He tries gleefully to tell them "what a commotion this will cause in the town. The whole water system will have to be overhauled." And he rubs his hands again. (Right up to the fifth act Ibsen uses this gesture as a leitmotif whenever Stockmann feels impelled to let his vitality reign unrestrained, whether for good or evil.) Brushing off his guests' congratulations and "walking up and down gleefully," he dismisses his alertness as no more than "duty." "I was a treasure seeker—and I struck lucky!" With a shout of "Hurrah!" he exits, bringing the first act to a close.

Was there any mention of the danger that would threaten guests coming to the spa in search of health? Only when Stockmann encounters official resistance, only when he is forced to back up his enthusiasm for bringing his influence to bear and for battling, for shaping the "fermenting substance" of the future by reasons that can be rationally accepted, does he recognize this danger as a compelling argument. The very quality that distinguishes him—his fixity of purpose— already caricatures him. It suggests rashness, a failure to stop and think. He blunders through the play exactly as Ibsen presents him in the first scene—a man driven by vigorous appetites. His life begins in staleness and deprivation and strives toward freshness and abundance; it seeks exuberance.

Stockmann enthusiastically accumulates property, resists privation of any kind, and refuses to have any part in the modest needs of the common man. He wallows in feelings of single-mindedness, for to him antitheses are unthinkable. He offhandedly exposes his moods, emotions, and wishes, as if there could be no resistance to his high-spirited, audacious enterprises. Decisions are more in his line than distinctions. The aspirations that drive him are neither socially nor morally motivated; they are an expression of his excessive vitality. They do, however, have a social and moral effect, for with his exuberant forwardness he bombards officials and newspapers with letters, articles, and memoranda, trying to put his projects, which he has hatched out "like an eider duck" (an expression that clearly indicates his instinctive nature) at the service of society. He pays no heed to practical methods, the choice of the right moment for action, or facts that have to be reckoned with. Ibsen did not fail to point out the narrowness of Stockmann's consciousness. No less than four times he shows him so emotionally excited that he forgets the maid's name, and never does he use it.

Why was Ibsen so drawn to a man like this? Because no one could be more effective than Stockmann, whose ideas stem from the irrational, for launching an assault on the rationalizations of a society that camouflages vested interests as common weal. Precisely by pursuing his projects wholeheartedly, "with ardent enthusiasm," without regard for property or family, Stockmann brings to the surface the material interests underlying the pretended concern with health and progress. He demonstrates the insincerity of bourgeois society; yet we must not forget that he is used by Ibsen throughout the play to serve himself as an illustration.

Stockmann is a progressivist by nature, so to speak; he has a creative enthusiasm for new realities. He brings this almost sensual delight in productive activity to bear on the task of getting the water pipes relaid. But his productivity fails in its purposes. It stems from bodily states, is rooted in private assumptions, and is given impulsive and heedless expression. Briefly, it is too spontaneous to be linked with society, which, as Marx says, always presents a historically developed relationship between nature and individual. Stockmann's tendency to regard reality as a raw fact that feeds his élan gives him a fresh, nonideological appeal, but his vanguardism is as strong as his awareness of any given situation is weak. His undeniable tinge of provincialism makes him informal and frankly unconventional, but it also gives him a plebeian awkwardness and tactical clumsiness. He is temperamentally incapable of understanding the social reality in which power and property are acquired and defended and conflicts of interest fought out. He recognizes no class structures, harbors no ideological suspicions; therefore, he mistakes opportunism for conviction, and unity of interest for "brotherly community." This man, whose conduct toward himself and others is guileless, is effectively made to recognize the force operative in a society. This happens in the second and third acts.

Stockmann's first and toughest opponent is his brother, mayor and chairman of the town council. The dialectic the play develops derives from the brothers' contrasting temperaments, which inevitably lead them into conflict—proof that Ibsen thinks in terms of characters even when this reduces the conflicts to a private, accidental level. So far as naturalness is concerned, the mayor is the very opposite of the doctor. A sufferer from dyspepsia, he fusses over himself with the untrusting watchfulness so characteristic of those with that ailment. Since he belongs to the established powers, his appetites have long been satisfied. He is therefore bent on stigmatizing his brother's unruly urge for self-realization and thoughtless desire for worldly goods as a threat to established order, while he canonizes vested interests as the common good, and the social hierarchy as "the well-ordered community."

This opposition of temperaments thus points to fundamental issues: the conflict between ideological rigidity and blind action and the interplay between "head" and "heart." These last two terms point to the mayor's reactionary mentality, which is focused on privilege and status, and to Stockmann's willful progressiveness, which improvises its goals and is without rational procedure because he conceives moral decision as a spontaneous outpouring of universal brotherhood. Thus, the two forces that might produce a community capable of mediating between the individual and society are struggling against each other.

Stockmann is the only one of the central characters who lives in a non- or preideological community—the family. Ibsen chose a family setting for the exposition of Stockmann's character, and the fifth act will take him back to the family setting. For a long time Stockmann fails to see the absurdity of his tendency to interpret social situations on the model of family relations, and to see that other characters are thinking and acting in accordance with their social functions or the ideological groups they represent. Nevertheless, Stockmann at first finds allies to support his project, though they do so out of common interests rather than common motives. These are Hovstad and Billing on the one hand, and Aslaksen, owner of the press, on the other.

These men are the spokesmen for two social forces, and they reflect the dispositions and tendencies of the two brothers. Hovstad and Billing, like the doctor, are progressive, "thirsty for action," and hungry for the future; they are passionately involved in public affairs. Aslaksen is the chairman of the home owners' association and an active member of the temperance society. Like the mayor, he enjoys a "position of some authority" through his various official positions. He is dedicated to the "cause of moderation," not because he is interested in bringing fresh, vigorous forces into action but simply because he wants to acquire power and manipulate the intellectual and economic means at his disposal to his own advantage.

The parallels, which extend from clothing, diction, and gesture to similarities of temperament, are so striking that it seems obvious which characters will rally around which brother. But Ibsen arouses this expectation only to disappoint it; he intends to make us aware of man as "the sum of all social factors" (to quote Brecht). Hovstad, Billing, and Aslaksen do not act in response to their individual endowment or to libidinously centered initiative. They act with an eye to economic conditions and power politics. The reactionary Aslaksen prints the liberal *People's Messenger*; the progressive newspapermen have to come to terms with him because they cannot print the paper on credit anywhere else. To attract readers, Hovstad, dedicated to "the fight for freedom and justice" and "the education of man through self-government," wants to publish a story implying that human destinies rest with a "supernatural power." Billing, an avowed revolutionary, is secretly trying to get himself appointed secretary of the town council. Aslaksen's heart puts him "on the side of the people," but his head draws him toward the local power bloc. They are all compromisers. Behind the back of the individual, as Marx put it, they all contribute to the survival of the dominant forms of social thought and life.

At first, however, the progressives and the law-abiding citizens support Stockmann's project of installing a new water system. The journalists support him because his discovery will be a trump card in their campaign to expose the infallibility of the established powers as superstition and to emancipate the oppressed. Aslaksen supports him because the home owners, whose livelihood depends on the baths, are bound to set great store by impeccable sanitary standards and because he hopes to remind the authorities—"with the

utmost moderation, of course"—of the influence of
the "compact majority" of the middle class, which
stands behind him.

But the mayor has no trouble in getting them to
reverse themselves. He only needs to present the cost
of the proposed new installation. The taxpayers would
have to raise hundreds of thousands of crowns, and the
baths would have to be closed for two years. The property owners are not prepared to support a program
that would restrict their profits; the progressive newspapermen cannot risk sponsoring a project that will
cost their readers money. It is curious that a matter
that calls for a moral stance should from the first be
seen exclusively from the economic and political points
of view.

The conversion of Stockmann's allies takes place in
the third act—in the editorial room of the newspaper.
Stockmann comes bursting in, impatient to see the
proofs of his article, which vociferously attacked the
obstructive authorities and called for action. The
mayor has hurriedly taken cover in the next room,
leaving behind his cap and staff of office in his hasty
retreat. Stockmann, still living in a "happy daze," has
no idea that the "dear, faithful friends," who had so
misread the economic picture as to think that his plans
promoted their interests, have had a change of heart. As
he indulges in visions of the tremendous demonstrations
of support awaiting him, his eye falls on his brother's
cap and official staff. Carried away by a triumphant
illusion, he dons the insignia of power, pompously
summons his brother into the editorial office, and
parades about as "authority" and "master of the town"
until the true situation dawns on him and cuts short
his hour of official glory.

This scene undoubtedly presents all the formal characteristics traditionally used to define peripeteia. As

Aristotelian dramatic doctrine prescribes, Ibsen has
timed it for the middle act, having followed just as
closely the classical pattern of the rising action through
exposition and climax. But the Aristotelian model does
not lend itself sufficiently to the social situation of
his time. As we shall see in this play, the peripeteia
does not, strictly speaking, introduce a catabasis; it
does not even lead up to a solution, tragic or comic.
And the peripeteia itself is removed from its true
function.

Instead of producing a sudden change in the hero's
destiny, it forces him into the belated realization that
his fate has changed under the impact of economic
factors. Since his consciousness lags behind reality, his
defiance (with which the audience morally identifies)
becomes at least partly comic. It is disturbing that
Stockmann's very nonconformity, pathetic as it may
be, and the spontaneity that has held out against circumstances, should become ridiculous. Ibsen shows this
very ironically. Stockmann's wife, who has hitherto
advocated moderation and kept his extravagance in
check for the sake of their own material interests, now
relinquishes her caution to stand by her husband without any reservation. The audience cannot take one side
or the other. The illusory nature of Stockmann's self-
understanding has been exposed; so has the falseness
of the other side's allegedly moral position. Thus the
reversal does not precipitate a resolution of the drama;
rather, Ibsen uses the reversal to establish distance
from both hero and society. If the play is to proceed in
the traditional five-act pattern, it must confine itself
to proving the impossibility of deriving drama from
this antagonism between hero and society.

In fact, in the last two acts Ibsen shows how the
characters become more and more inextricably
entangled in the positions they assumed in Act III.

(This is why the critics so often dismiss the fifth act as a coda, without looking into the reasons why this should be so.) The polarities are intensified to an almost unbearable degree. As the dramatic action diminishes, didactic elements come to the fore. Ibsen demonstrates the psychology of the outsider and the fanatical majority. Stockmann steps up his diatribes intended to expose the corrupt social order to a pitch of pointless frenzy. Society defends itself through ostracism and boycott against the uncompromising moral challenge that is bound to jeopardize it. Stockmann is able to make his explosive diatribe to the public only because Captain Horster allows him to use a room in his house. Even before he begins to speak, the meeting is cleverly manipulated by the mayor and his accomplices, who declare themselves "the voice of the majority." Aslaksen is elected moderator of the discussion by acclamation. They pay tribute to one another as guardians of the public welfare, even of the personal welfare of Stockmann. They brand the doctor as a revolutionary and, before the assembly can make up its mind, persuade it that he "has public opinion against him."

Then Stockmann bursts out in a violent indictment of society. Ibsen never wrote a more ruthless denunciation of the lying morality of the bourgeoisie, the anachronism of its dogmatically rigid norms, the enslaved conformity of its adherents than in this diatribe of Stockmann's. At last the problem seems to have been posed in decisive and purely moral terms. But it is not so. This unmasking is so hopelessly mixed up with the urgings of Stockmann's natural spontaneity and stems so obviously from his latent violence that its moral integrity is broken and distorted. His speech is wildly extravagant, full of intellectual wilfulness, overloaded with images, trailing off into banality and then rising again to moving heights.

The climax of the speech is a denunciation of "the compact majority," which he himself once identified with. Its only purpose is to scoff; it has no partner in dialogue and seeks none. Its aim is not consensus or the establishment of moral norms; it is merely preparing the way for the canonization of its own standpoint. Its language has a prophetic ring: "They must be exterminated like vermin—all men who live on lies! You will poison the whole country!" It also does not shrink from blasphemous allusions: "I do not say 'I forgive you, for you know not what you do.' " The assembly, bent on retaliation, pays Stockmann back in his own coin. It brands as a heretic the renegade who has indicted its mode of life, gets rid of him by unanimously declaring him "an enemy of the people." Only a drunk man who keeps making a disturbance in the back of the room, repeatedly thrown out and arguing his way back in, remains immune. He accepts Stockmann's aspersions with morose indignation, but he is the only man to vote against the censure.

With malicious irony, Ibsen has brought it home to us that except for this drunk, who is unsusceptible to the excesses of absolutism, no one shows any spirit of mediation. Society, rigidified in ideologies or concerned with inventing moral window dressing for profit- and power-seeking motives, falls into line against the outsider and reveals its own totalitarian, antihumane nature. Stockmann and his daughter lose their positions; his lease is canceled; his two sons are expelled from school. Demonstrators throw rocks at his house (the setting of Act V), doing serious damage. Totalitarianism betrays itself most clearly in society's effort to wage the battle by means of tactics of moral ostracism against the nonconformist who opposes the opportunism of the majority.

Stockmann has, of course, invited his ostracism, because his character has an antisocial trait, long concealed but called forth again by the heat of battle. He is not at ease with complex organization, which requires giving both sides their due. Anyone he encounters is either his friend or his enemy. So Stockmann's natural social sphere is the family. His acts and thoughts stem from his innate excessiveness and from his uncontrolled vitality. His desire for brotherly solidarity, as well as the impulsive initiative that realizes itself in his projects, prevents him from adjusting to a social role that would make him a part of the complicated structure of society as a whole.

Stockmann's desire to buy a primeval forest or a South Sea island and his wholesale scoffing at all majorities indicate his contempt for the phenomenon of society. The revolution he wants would end in rule by aristocracy. All this makes it doubtful whether his actions, the object of which is seemingly the realization of morality, can be called moral. If, that is, one defines the moral as being able to see one's own actions rationally at a distance, with an awareness of the alternative to one's own preferred direction. This approach is incompatible with Stockmann's absolutism.

Yet since the closed society must, after all, regard the outsider as a troublemaker who questions its sanctimonious image of itself, and since its pseudomoral ideology does not proscribe the promotion of vested interests but only cloaks it, that society perseveres in its attempt to bring Stockmann to heel or even make use of him. Or, it tries, as the mayor does, to find a way to cast suspicion on Stockmann's protest against the politics of vested interests posing as public welfare by implying that the protest itself is dictated by his own material advantage.

With the capital he had promised to leave to Stockmann's wife and children, his father-in-law, Morten Kiil, buys up stock in the baths for practically nothing, hoping in this way to blackmail Stockmann into retracting his story. When the newspapermen and Aslaksen hear of this transaction, they assume that Stockmann has spread the rumor that the medicinal springs are contaminated in order to acquire the stock cheaply through his father-in-law. Hoping to cash in on Stockmann's apparent financial coup, they offer him their newspaper and influence for propagating his views—for a price. But this attempt to bring Stockmann to his senses through self-interest rather than self-knowledge and self-control is bound to fail. Stockmann accepts the ruin of his family. He sends his father-in-law a calling card on which he has written "three large no's." He chases the journalists and the printer out of the house with a stick.

It is no accident that the visiting card should suggest a sleight of hand or that the expulsion of the journalists should recall another expulsion—the one from the Temple. In a brief interval the hosannas hailing the friend of the people have given way to the reviling cry of "Crucify him!" Threatened by pogrom, Stockmann is inclined, in the darkness of his unconscious, to see his fate as martyrdom. (This tendency is already obvious in his diatribe at the public meeting.) He sees Kiil, Hovstad, and Aslaksen as devils incarnate or as "emissaries of the devil." He rejects blackmail and friendly advances as temptations and undertakes to create society anew with "twelve youngsters." And indeed he is not entirely wrong, however much this interpretation may conflict with his self-understanding.

Society's persecution of him, extending even to ston-
ing, is totalitarian inasmuch as it uses the tactics of
religious ostracism.

Stockmann, a man with no talent for dialectics or
for considered action, a man who never achieves freedom of action, is not cut out to be a tragic hero. On the
other hand, he does not belong to a society that might
make this comic hero aware of his insufficiencies, thus
maneuvering him toward maturity. Ibsen leaves him
hanging in the balance between saint and fool. What
makes him look so harebrained is indeed his assump-
tion that he is a saint. Since he can be neither destroyed nor bought off, the play is open-ended. He has
made another "great discovery," one of those discov-
eries that give him a chance to develop his strained,
unreflective nature to the full: "The strongest man in
the world is the man who stands alone." The ending of
the play fixes him in the tragicomic ambivalence to
which Ibsen has exposed him:

Mrs. Stockmann (*smiling and shaking her
head*): Oh, Thomas!
Petra (*grasping his hands trustingly*): Father!

The Wild Duck

The theatrical basis of *The Wild Duck* is, in a complex way, nondramatic. Ibsen faces the task of explaining through dialogue characters who use speech as a means of self-concealment, a way of giving facts an ideological slant, distorting experience, and evading self-knowledge. He must develop dialogue between characters who treat conversation purely as a means of staging monologue to look like dialogue and force their "partners" into the cues that will enable them to continue their soliloquies. (On the other hand, they declaim these monologues in such a way as to empha-size their need for response.) Ibsen also has to set in motion a dramatic action between people whose exist-ence rests on a tacit agreement to avoid all decisions, all questioning of the established pattern of life and modes of existence, and all serious consideration of their possible perfectibility.

Since the characters (especially Hjalmar Ekdal, who, according to classical criteria, is the hero) never reveal themselves through words or actions, Ibsen is obliged to invent direct as well as indirect and devious ways of presenting them and involving them in dialogue and action. He therefore engages his figures in a network of constellations and parallel situations. He forces them to repeat, quote, and even contradict themselves. This method of characterization rests fundamentally on unmasking. Its aim is not to let the dramatic action synthesize the characteristic traits of the individual figures into a personality but rather to disintegrate these figures. To reveal their falseness to their own nature, their lack of self-realization, and the emptiness of their words and actions, Ibsen shows them in various different lights, which suggest comparisons and contrasts.

As the audience is trying to puzzle out these characters, especially Hjalmar Ekdal, Ibsen comes to its help with arguments between two supporting characters, Gregers Werle and Dr. Relling, whose commentaries provide a basis for interpreting the dramatis personae. They furnish the data and details that cannot be presented on stage because the characters have obliterated them from their reality. This method does not by any means indicate artistic weakness. By involving Gregers and Relling in mutual antagonism, Ibsen dramatizes them and converts their arguments into dramatic action. They are also fully integrated into the structure of the play. Their ultimate purpose is not to interpret the other characters but rather to respond to the opportunity the others offer them to air their own opinions. Argument is merely their way of simplifying reality to fit an ideological life program so as not to have to take it seriously. Yet Ibsen does not reduce these two arguers to a nonartistic function. They are not mere tools. In an indirect, that is, artistic, way he utilizes their method in founding their existence on their being *raisonneur* types.

We may take the figure of Gregers Werle as our

starting point. He sets in motion a drama whose partic-
ipants have long been in the habit of reifying human
conflicts, by reducing them to terms of money, or
evading them through lies and false solutions. Since the
drama cannot be derived from the characters of people
like this, what is needed to stir up a dramatic action is
an intriguer. Gregers, then, is an intriguer, even though
he may be motivated by moral claims. His morality is,
as Nietzsche would say, of nonmoral origin. Gregers
is the son of Consul Werle, merchant and owner of a
foundry. Since the death of his mother seventeen years
ago, he has been separated from his father and has
worked as a laborer in the mines owned by the consul
in Hoïdal in northern Norway.

The contempt for his father, instilled into him by his
mother from earliest childhood, has driven Gregers to
a life of loneliness and deprivation. His parents' marriage was an unhappy one. The consul had married
Gregers's mother for money and betrayed her by turning to other women, the last of whom was his housekeeper, Gina Hansen. Gregers's hatred of his father
was intensified by the ruthlessness with which the consul drove his partner, Lieutenant Ekdal, into bankruptcy and prison, as a result of which Ekdal's son
Hjalmar, Gregers's boyhood friend and a student of
great promise, was reduced to poverty. The partnership
broke up when an illegal business transaction, in which
Ekdal was innocently involved but for which Werle
was actually responsible, came to light. The consul put
the whole blame on the lieutenant and remained
unscathed himself, subsequently acquiring great
wealth and position. Werle then ruthlessly manipulated the lives of the people he had driven to the mar-
gins of society. He talked Hjalmar into marrying Gina,
who was pregnant with his own child. Since Gina is a

skilled retoucher, he set Hjalmar up as a photographer. When the lieutenant was released from prison, he found him copying jobs, for which he overpaid him.

So much for the prehistory. Ibsen outlines it dramatically in the first act by letting Gregers, who has been summoned to town to discuss the future of the business with his father, recapitulate the consul's role in the past and discover firsthand what happened to the Ekdals. The next four acts show how, at Gregers's instigation, this prehistory catches up with Hjalmar and Gina Ekdal, who, with Old Ekdal and their fourteen-year-old daughter Hedvig, have sought refuge in an illusory world of nonreality. They are all still living under the spell of catastrophic experiences—bankruptcy and the loss of social position and prestigious occupation. These experiences are catastrophic because they force into the open their latent feeling that "life is not worth living." Their bankruptcy destroys the social pattern of life in which they had felt secure and in whose terms they understood themselves. Overnight it has shown them that their former honor, recognition, and influence were based on reified reactions; they were not rooted in man's being but in the social roles he fills. They have acquired the feeling that personality is linked not to what a person is officially and specifically certified to be but to detachable attributes that are at man's disposal as furnishings of the self. They are therefore bound to consider loss of these attributes as a loss of self, even though only subconsciously.

Kierkegaard has described with extraordinary insight how people respond to this experience of nonbeing, to the realization that they are but a reflection of social circumstances. They make a desperate attempt not to be themselves. In the figure of Lieutenant Ekdal, Ibsen creates a dramatic portrayal of this desperate attempt to avoid the self-realization that is within one's grasp when all one's roles have been declared bank-rupt. Once released from prison, Old Ekdal thinks of nothing but regaining the attributes that used to dis-guise him as a personality—his uniform and his hunt-ing. Now that these personality attributes are no longer even part of a socially recognized role, their reified, meaningless nature is revealed more clearly than ever. The locale of the hunt is now the attic; the uniform is only worn for family celebrations.

Consul Werle draws a seemingly opposite conclu-sion, which is certainly no less self-destructive. Realiz-ing that functions, roles, and attributes make and unmake the personality, he assumes the right to make himself master of other people's fates. He rearranges the lives he has disrupted in accordance with the arbi-trary will of his self, his supreme authority. Since he is aware that society turns man into a commodity, he commercializes his relations with other people and reduces man to a victim of circumstances. Wanting at all cost to keep Gina's illegitimate pregnancy secret, he forces Hjalmar into a marriage and a profession in which he cannot realize himself. Of course, the more his power and reputation increase, the more he under-mines himself as a personality. Like Old Ekdal, he be-lieves that moral and spiritual results may stem from magical forces. The following lines illustrate this ten-dency they hold in common:

> Consul Werle: Let's hope no one noticed, Gregers . . . we are thirteen at table.

> Ekdal [after Hedvig's suicide]: The forest is tak-ing its revenge.

Gregers, on the other hand, seems to have drawn the right conclusion from what he has seen of the lying masquerade of social role-playing. He drops out of the social system and extricates himself from the consul's attempt to commercialize even the father-son relationship. Moreover, he questions the very basis of society, which he intends to expose as a "tragicomic farce." But looking more closely, we see that Gregers is "a complicated case." He is "ugly," at odds with himself: "But when a man is doomed to be Gregers Werle here in this world, as I am. . . ."

This conflict is his ruin. While he seems to reject all roles that would link him with the masks of society— the position to which his station entitles him, marriage, even sonhood—he refrains from taking the final step to self-realization, which is recognizing himself as a man whose being is at stake. He is constantly searching for a "task in life," and this task, which provides him with the "claim of the ideal," forces him back into his role, the last role he thinks he can play with a clear conscience. It gives him the opportunity "desperately not to be himself." For this task in life does not free him to be himself but reduces his selfhood to a stereotyped behavior, which becomes fixed in two ways. His "claim of the ideal" is his answer to the childhood shock caused by his mother's revelation of his father's infidelities. Thus he clings to an adolescent ideal through which he questions his patriarchal father and—through a process of identification—male-dominated society as well. The adolescent character of his absolute claim is tragicomically borne out by the fact that only Hedvig, who is little more than a child herself, takes him seriously.

Gregers is fixed in his boyhood; the infantility and lack of self-realization that mark both the consul and the lieutenant are also evident in him. More than that, he has disastrously tied his self to the "claim of the ideal." This is the foundation on which he bases his existence. The thing, the claim, is more important to him than the people it challenges. For this reason his relation to other people is also predetermined by non-personal factors; in other words, it is reified. Gregers has betrayed his freedom for the sake of the auto-matic workings of the cause to which he is given over. Whatever the cause demands, that he must do. This is why he makes the claim anywhere and everywhere, without regard for the people it is supposed to save. This is why he distorts Hjalmar into an idol to justify his claim of the ideal. This is why he forces Hedvig, who will die of it, to recognize it.

His thinking no longer embraces the human being. Just as the "lie of society" distorts other people's consciousness, the "task in life" distorts his. As the conclusion of the play shows, he is no longer capable of experiences that might break the fixation of his consciousness and his self. This is what I meant when I said that Gregers's morality is of nonmoral origin. One of the many tragicomic aspects of the play is that Gregers, whose self is hardened and whose concept of truth serves self-deception, sets the drama in motion and presses for openness.

The five acts of the play take place on three separate days: the first and second in the late afternoon and evening of the first day, the third and fourth on the morning and afternoon of the second, and the fifth in the early morning of the third day. Acts I and II, like Acts III and IV, are closely connected. Hence, the breaks, which are intended to articulate content and structure, coincide with the units of natural time—the days. While the dramatic events seek to show man as a "painted corpse" and the world he lives in as "white-washed graves," that is to say, while our minds are led in a counterclockwise direction, Ibsen is constantly reminding us of the passing of objective time. Since

the people within the Ekdal family are not subject to
the law of time, the passage of time could only be
presented as the passage of clock time. These people,
who are incapable of repeating their pasts and developing a future out of the present, must act against a
background of inexorably elapsing time, which shows
up the static nature of their lives in sharp contrast.

The shifts in space and time linking Acts I and II,
through which the lapse of time becomes actually measurable, serve this purpose, as do the stage directions
preceding the last three acts, which all mention a
change in the daylight, and the frequent references
from the second act on to Hedvig's approaching birthday. (In view of the "dis-illusioning" tenor of the play,
it is significant that her birthday, the coming of which
is so stressed throughout three acts, should be the day
of her death.) The same visual representation of the
passage of time is served by the curious opening of
Act IV. Gina is seeing off a newly married couple who
are standing "outside the door," unseen by the audience. Between the acts they have had their photo-
graphs taken; otherwise, they seem to have no dramatic
function. Obviously, time is passing more swiftly. Acts
I and II, which depict a late afternoon and evening,
sometimes deal twice with the same interval of time.
In Acts III and IV time flows consistently in one direction, but in addition to the time actually accounted for
they must suggest the passage of a whole day. Act V
moves with the steady flow of objective time and also
confines itself to the time interval actually depicted.

The thrust of the play is toward unmasking, especially the unmasking of Hjalmar Ekdal. To make it
effective, Ibsen first allows the figures to present themselves with their masks and disguises on, shows
them from false perspectives, permits deception. He
does this first by presenting the opening scene from

the point of view of the servants, who simplify and dis-
tort the facts without actually falsifying them. Furthermore, in the first three acts he presents Hjalmar
predominantly from the point of view of Gregers,
Gina, and Hedvig, who romanticize him into an idol
because they look up to him in the light of absurd or,
for that matter, merely commonplace expectations.
Only from the fourth act on, when Relling's sharp,
sober voice becomes increasingly audible, are these expectations deflated and the people who cherish them
exposed as illusionists.

The most effective factor in Ibsen's treatment of the
unmasking process is the interlinking of the first and
second acts. The first act takes place in Consul Werle's
house, where a party is being given to celebrate
Gregers's arrival from Hoïdal. At Gregers's suggestion,
Hjalmar has been invited. Act II is set in the Ekdals'
attic studio. The two acts are connected in several
ways. Three characters—Old Ekdal, who, to everyone's embarrassment, has had to leave the consul's
locked office by way of the living quarters, then
Hjalmar and Gregers—leave the evening party one
after the other at irregular intervals. Then, at more or
less the same intervals, they make their entrances in
Act II, which has opened with only Gina and Hedvig
on stage. These connections, which show the characters in different lights, relativizing their modes of behavior, create the setting for the unmasking. Of course,
Ibsen skillfully sets the process in motion even within
the first act, by changing the composition of the con-
versational groups, for instance.

At the beginning of the play he systematically shows
Hjalmar in false colors. In Act I he presents Hjalmar
in a milieu where his dilettantish attitude to life is
either not recognizable or can be put down to social
awkwardness, because his characteristic habits of life

do not come into play and because, apart from one
exception, his words do not have to be borne out by
actions. Ibsen also lets Hjalmar introduce himself as he
replies to Gregers's questions about what he has been
doing in the seventeen years since they last met. In
other words, he presents him from the falsest possible
perspective. Hjalmar's rapid changes of pose confuse
the audience, until Ibsen effectively brings the game to
an end in the second act. As soon as he gets home,
Hjalmar exchanges the dress coat he has worn to the
consul's for his "loose, comfortable house jacket," that
is, for the garb of the sentimental, coddled husband
and father. In this way Ibsen arouses our suspicions
that Hjalmar may borrow feelings and opinions as
readily as he has borrowed the dress coat of Molvik, the
onetime theology student.

And, indeed, Ibsen begins the exposure in the second part of Act I. The conversation with Gregers
that we have already mentioned gives Hjalmar the
opportunity to pose in various roles, the first of which
is the self-sacrificing son. He is unmasked when he
repudiates his shabbily dressed father. (As the play
goes on, Ibsen will use discrepancy between word and
deed as his principal means of exposure.) Hjalmar next
presents himself in the role of husband, "eager to set
up his own household," only to be exposed, in the
argument between the consul and Gregers at the end
of the act, as a helpless fool who has been tricked into
a marriage not only beneath him but also, by bourgeois
standards, dishonorable and into a line of work for
which he is quite unsuited. Ibsen omits mention of
the third role that might give him some prestige—the
role of father.

Not until the beginning of the second act does the
audience learn that Hjalmar has a daughter; and
Gregers does not know it until the middle of this act.

Thus, we first see Hjalmar the father from the illusion-istically distorted, expectant viewpoint of Hedvig. As the style and inner form of this play dictate, the very modest anticipation with which Hedvig is awaiting her father's return is unfulfilled. Hjalmar's behavior in the first and second acts shows that the chief factor in his relationship to his daughter is forgetfulness. In Act III we shall see that he has also forgotten his promise to read books with her. So when Gregers comes to his studio and he goes into his father act, it has already been discredited.

The interplay between the first two acts initiates two more unmaskings. The whole network of lies of the Ekdal family is revealed through the contrast of the first two acts. The seemingly tranquil family scene at the Ekdals' after Hjalmar arrives home parallels Gregers's bitter argument with the consul. By inviting comparison, the parallel brings home to us the reality of the Ekdal family's closeness resting on lies and self-deceptions. While conflicts in the Werle family are angrily fought out, the Ekdals try to suppress them. Hjalmar's disrespect for his father is ignored. Hedvig's disappointment at Hjalmar's letting her down is hushed up with a few tears. Old Ekdal's escape into alcohol is charitably glossed over.

To achieve the second unmasking, Ibsen uses another artistic device. In Act II he has Hjalmar quote a scene from Act I. Again and again Ibsen places his characters in the ambiguous light of a double perspec-tive. Usually he strips off the masks of sham personality through the gradual revelation of the past; in other words, he destroys the deliberately created legend. Here, however, the audience actually witnesses the moment when a man begins to create a pose to disguise his lack of character. Hjalmar presents his humiliation by the servants in the consul's home as a triumph. Or, to be more exact, by the clever use of words he induces his family to create this false interpretation for him.

In Acts III and IV, when Gregers tries in the name of the "claim of the ideal" to force Old Ekdal out of what Ludwig Binswanger calls the traps of life and into reality and to force the marriage of Hjalmar and Gina out of lies and into truth, Ibsen depicts Hjalmar in even more vivid colors. But to get an undistorted view of these characters of Ibsen's who are living out their lives in self-deception, one often has to come upon them from behind. This is the case here: the brightest light is shed upon Hjalmar retroactively, in the fifth act. At the end of the play the audience has an unobstructed backward view of him and his childhood. Relling reveals him from this angle, recalling how he was brought up by his aunts, "two hysterical old maids," who unfortunately believed him to have "a great mind." Relling reveals that from childhood Hjalmar had to accept a self that he could uphold only through pose and rhetoric, never in reality. And all of a sudden it becomes dreadfully clear that this childhood configuration still exists. Hjalmar still lives under the tutelage of two women who expect too much of him; he is still escaping from himself in lies.

Even more obviously than the other characters, Hjalmar is branded as having failed to attain self-realization. He has remained hollow and empty, far from self-realization, because in him the interplay between subject and object has never taken place. He has created no reality for his self, neither a human nor a material one. Hjalmar must always have two things at hand—his flute and his pistol. Of course, he has no mutual relationship with them; things could never influence him as forces possessing life of their own. He has reduced them to fetishes, possessing them instead of having an inward feeling for them. They make accessible to him emotional reactions that do not reside within him. They constitute his spiritual life. They provide a substitute for life's meaning as well as its threat. His handling of the pistol, especially, shows how he uses things to manipulate feelings.

His relationship to people works in the same way. Gina has no reality for him as a wife; like his aunts, she is just a mother substitute. The only time he confronts her as his wife—at the instigation of Relling— she rejects his words as "sayings." It is also characteristic that the motherly support on which he depends for security largely takes the form of plentifully buttered slices of bread. I have already showed that he does not relate to Old Ekdal and Hedvig as son and father. His reified attitude toward Hedvig becomes obvious when he learns that she is not his natural daughter. At this moment Ibsen offers Hjalmar an opportunity he gives to several of his characters: to appropriate, by free decision and the prompting of the heart, something that, according to the rigid law of the social code, does not belong to him. But Hjalmar rejects Hedvig. Like Old Ekdal, a pathetic example of shattered, senile existence, Hedvig, who is threatened by blindness, is no more to him than a source of self-assurance and sympathy, which provide him with some inner life.

Hjalmar is also incapable of relating self and outer world through language. To him, language is not a means of actualizing his self. He treats it as a vehicle for declamatory speeches and for enacting a character through cryptic quotations. His chief sources are the Bible and, after his "long walk" with Gregers, the jargon of "essential reality" through which Gregers deals with society. His language has nothing to do with self-expression; it lacks all nonsubjective reality. Its aim is not to present facts and circumstances in words but to dress up the real world with tricky effects or emotions in order to make it yield sympathy, particularly self-sympathy. "The old man with his silver hair"; "happy and carefree, chirping like a little bird, she flutters off into eternal night"—this is how he talks about Old Ekdal and Hedvig.

For Hjalmar, the whole world is just material for weaving dreams and lies. This criticism deserves to be taken seriously because it casts a suspicion on art. For Ibsen has made Hjalmar, like so many of his leading characters, something of an artist. As represented by Hjalmar, the artist would appear to be an illusionist who deliberately falsifies naked reality, a creator of metaphors that disguise reality. As Nietzsche said, art is more powerful than knowledge because art desires life.

Hjalmar, who likes to speak of himself in the third person, that is, to watch himself acting, has a masterly talent for seeing himself in imaginary roles. And Rel-ling gives him effective support. To help Molvik, the unsuccessful theology student, to achieve an inner life, Relling has talked him into assuming a demonic char-acter. It is significant that Molvik, with his pretended demonism, remains bound to the church that was once his home through his very negation of it, just as Gregers is chained to society through his "claim of the ideal." These are all attempts to regain through the back door a lost status that had guaranteed some mean-ing to life. And Relling, to whom "ideal" is only a synonym for "lie," has shown Hjalmar the way too. The "life-lie—the stimulating principle," which Relling has thought up for him, is that an important scientific discovery is gestating in Hjalmar. When it has been worked out, it will restore the Ekdal family to its lost social position.

While the consul has resocialized Hjalmar, Relling has remoralized him. But for Ibsen, any return to the

past spells ruin. It prevents the realizations that seem
to be within man's grasp when he can no longer rely
on society and tradition for support. And, of course,
Relling himself, who unmasks the lie as the principle
that makes existence possible at all, is just as far as all
the others from the freedom that permits self-realization. His unfulfilled love for the consul's housekeeper
(revealed in Act IV) tells the audience that he, too,
maintains self-deceptions to the very last and can overcome disillusionment only through anesthetizing himself. Here we recognize his lack of self-awareness and
alert thinking. His proclivity for unmasking is so inflexible because he hopes in this way to develop a position
and a fixed way of life in which to root his self, just
as Gregers wants to base his self securely on the "claim
of the ideal." No more than the others does Relling
seem to have a very clear understanding of his own
design for life.

To promote the Ekdal family's self-realization,
Gregers tries to destroy the network of lies and self-
deceptions in which the Ekdal family is entangled. But
he causes only destruction. The disintegration of the
marriage between Gina and Hjalmar finds a parallel in
the prospective marriage between the consul and his
housekeeper. Ibsen symbolizes the existence of Hjalmar
and Old Ekdal—mutilated, retreating from the coldness and nakedness of reality, utterly wretched—in the
image of the wild duck that the family has installed in
the attic, now transformed into an artificial nature
reserve. The wild duck, wounded by a shot from Consul Werle so that it "could no longer fly," plunged
down to the bottom and "bit itself fast in the tangle
and seaweed," never to come back up to the surface
again. Only an "amazingly clever dog" was able to
drag it out again. This is the role Gregers would like
to play in the Ekdals' life.

Gregers is least successful with Old Ekdal: at the first hint of the "claim of the ideal," he falls asleep. The effect he has on Hjalmar is perverted: the "claim of the ideal" provides him with a new vocabulary and a new role to hide behind for a while. Otherwise, the effect is limited to the various "arrangements" Hjalmar makes for a free and independent life, which end in the infantile regression to the plentifully buttered slice of bread that makes unnecessary all decisions.

Only with Hedvig is Gregers successful; and even this is a tragicomic, distorted success. Hedvig is not rigid and inflexible like the others; her instability is that of youth. In the hour that determines her destiny she learns that she is an illegitimate child; she is therefore unable to understand herself according to the standards of society. She too is related to the Flying Dutchman, a figure who haunts Ibsen's plays in many disguises, a man who roams the vast openness of the world, always in search of absolute self-fulfillment. To her more alert senses, what Gregers says sounds strange from the beginning. She realizes that his words make everything that used to seem unquestionable appear ambiguous. And deeply attached as she is to the wild duck (as its foster mother) she is ready to kill it as proof to her father of her readiness for sacrifice.

The fifth act shows how Hedvig is driven from the sacrifice of the wild duck into self-sacrifice. In a scene of magnificent grandeur Ibsen has effectively combined horror and mockery. He begins with the gesture of classical tragedy—sacrifice—but then distorts the catharsis of tragedy into tragicomedy. The scene leading up to the catastrophe is set as comedy, with the exchange of roles and masks. Hedvig has secretly gone up to the attic to act out the part intended for Old Ekdal: to kill the wild duck with a shot from the pistol. In the adjoining studio she can hear Hjalmar and

Gregers playing out a farcical comedy based on false
suppositions. Both of them believe that it is Old Ekdal
who is moving around in the attic. Hjalmar thinks he is
caring for the bird as he does every day, while Gregers
believes that he is about to shoot it at Hedvig's
request. Hjalmar, who, in his heroic role, has just
repudiated Hedvig and threatened to leave the house,
now changes roles to fit the new situation and melo-
dramatically assumes a sentimental one. Without
answering Gregers (as the stage direction specifically
states) he makes a tear-jerking bid for sympathy, pre-
tending to be afraid that Hedvig will give up her
childish belief in his talent in favor of a life of ease with
her rightful father, the consul.

Gregers for his part urges him on to one climax after
another, though unintentionally, because in this scene
Hjalmar is not looking for a partner in dialogue any
more than Gregers is acting as one. Gregers is really
serving as prompter for Old Ekdal, whom he supposes
to be in the attic. He lays great stress on Hedvig's
complete readiness for sacrifice in order to induce the
Old Ekdal to fire the longingly awaited shot. Hedvig
is confused by all this deception, self-deception, and
play-acting. She takes the alternating declamations
and cues for a conversation developing quite straight-
forwardly out of their state of shock. So when Hjalmar
says, in the tone of a man who despairs of humanity,
"If I were to ask her: Hedvig, are you willing to
renounce that life for me?", she shoots herself. Here
tragicomedy reaches its high point. Hjalmar is not
addressing to his daughter the question that Hedvig
answers so irrevocably; he is addressing it, in self-pity,
to himself. Moreover, a grotesque misunderstanding
has arisen. By "life" he means not existence itself but
the life of luxury that the consul could provide for
Hedvig.

The shot is greeted by the terribly inappropriate and deluded exultation of Gregers, whose mind is stuck in his fixed idea: "I knew it! I knew that he would be rehabilitated through the child!" Then comes the horror. But it is short-lived. Hedvig's sacrificial death has no purifying effect. Her gesture is meaningless, and over her dead body the others merely show how stubbornly they are identified with the sectarian narrow-mindedness of their self-deceiving roles, which are supposed to provide meaning and a sense of value to their existence. To them, Hedvig's death is just an occasion to hold on to their own unrealizable selves. Old Ekdal's reaction reveals the desire to escape most conspicuously. He "goes up to the attic and closes the door behind him." But the behavior of the others is motivated by the same desire. To Hjalmar, Hedvig's death serves as a subject for a declamation. Gregers preaches about the sublime. Relling uses the opportunity for unmasking. Molvik rattles off the burial service, thus assuming the role in which he once sought security for his life. Only Gina, whose honest, simple acceptance of life gives her a certain stature as the play progresses, stands up for Hedvig by refusing to allow the child's corpse to be "paraded" to gratify the others' need for self-assertion.

The Wild Duck, which weaves into a dramatic play a vicious circle of "painted corpses" and characters who misuse themselves for self-pity or self-admiration, is one of the greatest of Ibsen's works because it reveals the man who proclaims escape from all illusions to be yet another illusionary.

Rosmersholm

More than any other play of Ibsen's, *Rosmersholm* bears out György Lukács's point that modern drama is multidimensional because man's action and thought no longer derive from a "unified, metarational sense of the world." We are even justified in concluding that not only the universal validity of metarationality but even its very reality is being questioned. It follows that the characters in this play, at least the males, are doctrinaire: preachers, political partisans, pedagogues, and demagogues. Doctrine eliminates the problem. It relieves us of the obligation "to accept the burden of the idea," as Hegel said. The characters in *Rosmersholm* live in an age in which, according to Nietzsche, the highest values are being devalued. In this value vacuum, patterns of life flourish in which obsolete dogmas are anachronistically kept alive or new doctrines are mythologized and made supreme, stifling the tendency in life to acquire self-understanding through dialectical movement.

The dramatic action of the play consists mainly in the way Rosmer, a "renegade former pastor," acquires an undoctrinaire image of himself, which can accommodate the diversity of his personality. He acquires it by coming to terms, through dialogue, with his past and with those in whom, for him, the past lives on. In this play Ibsen's basic dramatic pattern is illustrated in a new form: man acquires self-consciousness and the ability to use his reason by overcoming the outdated dogma that binds him to "childhood faith," and a conception adequate to the self can be formed if the one-sided notions that belong to the past merge into the totality of the self.

Rosmer comes from a line of ancestors who have held positions as "clergymen and officers, state officials and high dignitaries, one and all." All of them served the institutions that for centuries have administered and dogmatized love, morality, and justice. The members of the family have long seen each other only as representatives of this tradition. This is the case with Rosmer, too. After his father chases his tutor, Brendel, off the estate with a whip for inculcating progressive ideas in his pupil, family tradition forces young Rosmer to become a pastor. He marries Beata, sister of Professor Kroll, a rigid conservative. It soon becomes clear that for Rosmer piety is only a means of satisfying his need for the existence of authority. By accepting the law as absolute validity, although at best the law merely lays down one possible type of moral obligation, he can submit to it. He regards marriage as a juridical rather than a moral relationship and zealously attacks Mortensgard, a teacher by profession, for living in a marriagelike relationship with a woman who has been rejected by her husband. As a result, Mortensgard is ostracized and dismissed from his position.

Rosmer's wife, Beata, who cannot have children, becomes an invalid after a few years of marriage and begins to waste away. She is nursed by Rebecca West,

a young woman from northern Norway. In the final
stage of her illness Beata's personality changes in a
disturbing way: she becomes sensual, free from inhibi-
tions. Apparently in a state of mental and spiritual confusion, she finally drowns herself in the millrace that
borders Rosmer's estate.

Rebecca, who had already assumed the "regency" of
the household while Beata was still alive, remains at
Rosmersholm as a "companion." A strangely spiritual-
ized relationship, based on camaraderie and exchange
of ideas, springs up between Rosmer and Rebecca. It
seems to be immune to reification through sexual or
economic possessiveness, the perversion Ibsen is so
quick to suspect in the relationship between man and
woman. Soon Rosmer falls under the influence of
Rebecca's liberal ideas. He breaks away from "sacred
prejudices" and resigns his position. Since he is unable
to bring himself to take sides openly, he retreats into
private life. Clearly, he has not overcome the past, at
least not in the misty realm of the irrational. Paralyzed
by an attack of superstitious fear, he does not dare to
cross the footbridge from which Beata threw herself
into the millrace.

So when the curtain rises, events hang in the balance.
Inwardly, inside his house, Rosmer has created a
sphere free from anachronisms. But his estate adjoins
the millrace. The past seems to be overcome. Rosmer
believes he can look at it calmly, having emerged from
it "invulnerable." And yet it threatens and attracts
him. It stands in his way and forces him to make
"detours," as if he were not free on his own land. As
though carrying out a ritual, he circles around the
place in which the past is so oppressively localized, but
he cannot exorcise its powers. He cannot do so because
he brackets it out and objectifies it, instead of destroy-

ing its anachronistically magical effect by making it contemporary and reliving it in the freedom and serenity that reason confers.

Like many of Ibsen's characters, Rosmer is schizoid: he is chained, in a compulsive, unenlightened dependency, to the past, while at the same time he engages in intellectual speculations ranging dreamily beyond the present to the man of the future. The dichotomy would be overcome in the utopia of "men of nobility" that he has dreamed up. This synthesis-seeking utopia would be based on the "inherent power" within each individual; its aim would be man's self-salvation. Its existence would depend on men who have "freed their thoughts and purified their will" and who "bear the moral law within themselves like a law of nature." The morality of the future would lose its categorical character and become identical with the spontaneity of the free act of will. It would be grounded in people who have reconciled their realities and their natures, who have freed their thoughts and purified their wills by divorcing them from all anachronistic, ideological, and egotistical motives. Rosmer reinforces this interpretation of society by insisting that "men of nobility" would necessarily be oriented to joy. The impulse of desire, as we know, becomes stilled in joy.

Joy is changed into its opposite through guilt. Man is fully aware of himself in joy. The man who has accumulated guilt, however, is chained to the past. Fearing to entangle himself in guilt, Rosmer does not put his speculations into practice. He does not openly advocate his utopia. He hides his change of mind from the dying Beata, for to opt for the "man of nobility" seems to him a repudiation of his ancestry and of those who share it. And he is convinced that the "man of nobility" can live only in the "quiet, joyful certainty of being free from guilt." This belief clearly reveals the utopian

character of his dream. To break the spell of the past,
he conceives a man divorced from history, because as
long as man is subject to the passage of time he is, at
any given moment, guilty toward himself. Rosmer also
fails to realize that guilt is the way by which man
attains self-realization. And because he remains undecided—although Rebecca urges him to make a decision
—he encourages the others to involve him in their
programs.

Meanwhile, the people in the outside world split into
two camps representing Rosmer's unreconciled tendencies: the conservatives, headed by Kroll; and the
progressive groups, led by Mortensgard, now editor of
the radical *Beacon*. Both of them want the prestige
that Rosmer's name would bring them. What they are
interested in is, of course, not Rosmer himself but the
qualities that are detachable from him because they
are merely external to him. They try to approach the
old Rosmer, who has outlived himself, counting on him
because they cannot get the undoctrinaire Rosmer,
who insists on man's autonomy, to serve their programs.

Kroll is the first to begin. He has not set foot in
Rosmersholm, a stronghold of conservatism, since
Beata's death, but now he appears, looking for com-
panionship. Kroll is more deeply and hopelessly mired
than Rosmer in the dishonesty that appears throughout
this play as anachronism. He is a fanatical legalist.
Like all fanatics, he rages against what Kant called
"the leaving behind of youth for which one is oneself
to blame," whether in himself or in others. He sacrifices
his freedom to law, because he sees the law as the most
reliable principle for giving the self a secure foundation
in heteronomy and stagnation, which resist reason and
change.

Kroll has lagged so far behind the passing of time,

which he should have used to make progress in, that he is lost to contemporaneity. Up to now, in both his spheres of life—his family and his school—he has enjoyed the exercise of authority that is the reward of the law to its compliant functionaries. Now, however, he exerts that authority only over the poor students. The students in his school and even his own children are imbued with "the spirit of revolt." This rebellious-ness naturally increases his fanaticism, because he sees the rebels seizing the freedom that so attracts him (though he represses its attraction out of fear). He has rationalized the immaturity of his self through legalism and projected his self-hatred into condemnation of the rebels. Like his pupils, he knows that codified tradition is just as opposed to self-consciousness as to the con-temporaneity of his time. But instead of making the effort to create a new reality, he escapes from the value vacuum into the anachronism of tradition.

Of course, Kroll does not get any support from Ros-mer. His dramatic function is to make Rosmer realize how deeply he has alienated himself from his back-ground and how little he has realized the future. Here we recognize the situation with which so many of Ibsen's plays open: the introverted utopian must be brought to confession, and the dreamer must be turned into an activist. Kroll gives Rosmer no choice: he is an effective maker of heretics. He sees to it that the uni-formity of the world, undialectically derived from dogma, sanctified to the point of unassailability, is not questioned. For this reason, he brands nonconformity as immoral and outlaws anyone who thinks differently. He has Rosmer publicly denounced in the conservative County Reporter and tries to damn him by represent-ing contemporaneity as a vice. Because he does not discuss the present but merely judges it by anachro-nistic standards, the only epithets at his disposal are formalistic, negative ones such as "rebel," "renegade," "turncoat," "evil character," "Judas," and "traitor." He sees movement and progressivism as desertion, not as healthy impulse.

Rosmer is thus forced to opt for his utopia seriously, in full knowledge of the consequences. Perhaps he has also realized that the future does not necessarily spring fully armed from the arsenal of the present but may have to be won by fighting back the past. Rebecca speeds up the process by a letter that brings Mortensgard to Rosmersholm. But before Rosmer can debate matters with him, Brendel crosses his path.

While Kroll has made the past an urgent presence, Brendel, the liberal, progressive tutor of Rosmer's boyhood, robs the future of all substantial shape. Ever since the day when his idealism cost him his position, Brendel has led the life of a vagabond and idler. The ideals that make man appear perfectible and commit him to their realization now absolve him from any serious act of will. Although ideals bring him into conflict with doctrinaire minds and the anachronistic constitution of society, they are stripped of their heuristic and speculative force. In a society bogged down in obsolete trivialities they serve as an excuse for disclaiming all responsibility.

Idealism, for Brendel, is emptied of all meaning and becomes no more than a way of escaping from the present into some vague, misty dreamland. Utopia comes to serve psychological purposes. It stimulates a sense of self, lends passion to the creative urge, which momentarily cloaks the dreamer's self-hatred. This is why Brendel describes the blissful state into which his fantasies transport him in a mixture of religious, erotic, and aesthetic terms. Ibsen takes this opportunity to expose idealism as a consumer product, just another means of escape from what György Lukács called "transcendental homelessness."

Brendel claims to be at "a turning point in his life." He wants to "take hold of life with a strong grip," to lay down his thoughts and ideas "on the altar of progress and freedom." But although he possesses "the idealist's talent for failing to know himself"—to use Nietzsche's sarcastic phrase—he must sense that his ideas, if put to the test, would disintegrate. His announced intention of joining the local temperance society "for a week or so" proves that he plans to become a serious, dependable worker for only a little while. The middle-class uniform he borrows from Rosmer—shirt with starched cuffs, overcoat, and boots —will not be worn for more than a couple of days.

Rosmer does not yet recognize his meeting with Brendel as a sardonically prophetic parody of the career of the utopian he bears within himself. He wants to use the radical newspaper to make his liberal views generally known and to win supporters for his vision of the future. But once again his past, which he believed he had shaken off by an act of will, is catching up with him. Mortensgard has no use for the "honesty of will" that has arisen in Rosmer since his "gods departed far away." Rosmer's defamation campaign has destroyed Mortensgard's integrity and moral spirit, just as Rosmer's father paralyzed Brendel's commitment to utopia.

Mortensgard has learned that it is unwise to oppose the ruling ideology. While he knows as well as Rosmer does that the church, as Nietzsche said, is only "God's sepulcher and tombstone," he does not leave the "house of corruption" to promote a "new revelation . . . or the revelation of something new" or—to use Bloch's words —to serve as "quartermaster for future man." He eval-

uates doctrines according to their effectiveness rather
than their truth. So it does not bother him that the
human mind remains fixed in anachronism. Unlike
Rosmer, he is committed not to synthesis, which would
mediate the conflict on a higher level of life, but rather
to compromise, which permits progressive ideas to be
interpreted in archaic terms. It is precisely this that
makes him, for Ibsen's satirical purposes, the man of
the future. He has the ability to do without ideals and
"never wills more than he can do."

Rosmer realizes that if he wants to abide by truth
and freedom he will be cast upon his own resources.
He summons up his courage for a decisive step. To
"get rid of the dead body on his back" and oppose to
the past "a new, living reality," he asks Rebecca to
become his second wife. Her assent might have been
liberating inasmuch as it might have transformed the
only seeming harmoniousness of their platonic relationship, whose natural, irrational aspect has been suppressed, into a union free of the instinctive element,
which determines man out of the preconscious depths
of the past. But Rebecca refuses the proposal with a
vehemence that is bewildering to Rosmer.

And so the past of Rebecca and Beata, up to now
glimpsed only when the spotlight fell on it in passing,
begins to be discussed. Kroll sets the revelation in
motion. Another of Ibsen's schemers, he has a genius
for skepticism because he wants to evade his fundamental doubt in his own existence. Suddenly, in the
light of Rebecca's past, he sees in her face what Hofmannsthal described as "the Medusa element in life."
Rebecca came from an obscure, illegitimate background and grew up in rough, scandalous circumstances. She is one of those characters of Ibsen's who
are driven by a primeval, pagan, Viking-like urge to

subjugate the world to their premoral selves. She also
has a troll-like talent for using her almost magical se-
ductiveness to make people submit to her immorality.

Rebecca tries to gain power over Rosmer in order
to participate through him in the freedom and scope
offered by the open-minded age about to dawn. She
hopes to do this by identifying herself without reservations with the "new thoughts and ideas," which will
shape the future of autonomous man as Brendel had
described it to Rosmer long ago. A sudden awakening
of passion for Rosmer strengthened the ruthlessness
with which she went to work. To free him from the
spell of his traditions, she drove Beata to suicide, making her believe, through hints and implied suggestions,
that she stood in the way of Rosmer's happiness and
future and that his opinions had already undergone a
secret change. Beata, too, showed symptoms of self-
hatred. She clung to Rebecca "with a sort of desperate
passion," through which she tried to give a positive
turn to her self-contempt. And so began the erosion of
her personality that will finally end in suicide.

In the world of ideologists and aestheticizing ide-
alists Rebecca is not as atavistic as she appears at first
glance. With her irresistible beguilements and seduc-
tiveness, she is a manifestation of the anachronism of
the world that smolders within her because the target
of her rebellion is law and "legalization" instead of
morality and moral instinct. Through Rebecca, late
bourgeois society, which is only superficially Christian,
falls victim to the demonic prehistoric forces it has
ignored and relegated to its fringes but never overcome. It could not overcome them because it preferred
hypocritical conservatism and meaningless utopianism,
which absolve man from the obligation to emancipate
himself, to a system of life based on freedom and truth,

which can only stem from responsibility and dialectical self-understanding.

The past has a threatening immediacy if it has not been reconciled with the present. The Austrian dramatist Hugo von Hofmannsthal described the process of self-realization as "binding and being bound." Rosmer was not ready to bind Rebecca—his opposite so far as family and background are concerned—until she was already hopelessly entangled in the chains of her destiny. It is true that since Beata's death Rebecca has not only liberated Rosmer to his self "inwardly as well as outwardly" but has herself been "purified and ennobled" to the very depths of her soul through her relationship with Rosmer. In the meantime, however, their guilt has grown to the point where they cannot break free of the past, although in their marriage Christian and pagan elements would combine in a higher uniformity.

Once again Brendel crosses the path of Rosmer and Rebecca, moving peripherally around the characters who struggle toward a false integration. Again his fate is to be seen as a prefiguration. He makes another appeal for transformation, but this time for a return "downhill . . . to the great nothingness." His ideals were a mask; behind them we see the nihilism out of which they were born. To Rosmer, too, the future seems to be undermined by emptiness and desolation. Again he is tempted, like all the other characters, to evade self-hatred by using others as a means of self-assertion or self-negation. To regain his faith in the purifying power of his utopia, he asks Rebecca to join him in making atonement for Beata's death through suicide. Only when she "joyfully" agrees "to take the road Beata took" does he finally succeed in overcoming a preoccupation with the magical through a moral decision. At last he rises to an emancipated point of view. He proclaims autonomous man to be the highest authority, endows him, once he attains self-awareness, with power over right and rite. Rosmer pronounces his own judgment and takes Rebecca in marriage, as his legitimate wife. Of course, this can be no more than freedom for death. To master the past through a free moral decision, the two lovers jump into the millrace from the bridge from which Beata went to meet death.

But we should not try to eliminate the ambiguity Ibsen intentionally gave to this ending. In any event, the future is the victim of the past. Ibsen gives the last word to Mrs. Helseth, the housekeeper of Rosmersholm: "The dead wife has taken them both." The suspicion is not dispelled that the lovers have succumbed to the magical, irrational force of the past and ideologized their past-dictated action into a moral act of sacrifice.

Hedda Gabler

In the four-act drama *Hedda Gabler*, Ibsen reveals the seeds of death in the union of two people. The union has been ratified as a marriage but has little possibility of being one. Indeed, it does not have the makings of any conceivable kind of human relationship. Jörgen Tesman, doctor of liberal arts and a leading candidate for a university chair shortly to be filled, and Hedda Gabler, daughter of the late General Gabler, are joined in this misalliance.

Ibsen presents them at the moment when the latent crisis is about to erupt. The curtain rises on the morning after their return from a six-month honeymoon. A marriage that is not permitted to realize its own values and the obligations deriving from it, or even to establish itself as a marriage at all, is reduced to a "doctrine of social prudence." Ibsen's contemporary, Kierkegaard, characterized such a marriage as "a rotation system," as a mode based on constant change. Travel, with its frequent "change of soil," offers man plenty of opportunities to live by the rotation system. When the traveling ends, a high-strung abundance of ingenuity is required if the game, an invitation to look away from one's self, is to continue. A time of crisis now looms for the newly-weds.

Another factor is even more important. Hedda is now pregnant, a condition which is to her a meaning-less physical occurrence—one that proclaims that a relationship based on interests in common, such as travel, is now a marriage, which will involve her in intimacies and obligations that she can never live up to.

Tesman himself escapes this critical conflict, partly because he is not yet aware of Hedda's pregnancy, but chiefly because he is quite incapable of the self-understanding that brings the self into conflict with social roles. Tesman, who lost his father and mother in early childhood, was brought up (like Hjalmar Ekdal in *The Wild Duck*) by two unmarried aunts—a sug-gestive hint. All the characters in this play, with the possible exception of Lövborg, Tesman's boyhood friend, are guilty of human inadequacy: they are incapable of a decisive, serious act of will. To put it another way, although they are capable of decisive action dictated by will, they cannot will seriousness.

Using the cast of *Hedda Gabler* as an example, one could set up a typology of this human inadequacy. The characters would be analyzed in terms of their ability to love, love being defined as the power that frees man to unlock himself, open himself, dare to come out in the open, and seriously and irrevocably will himself and his beloved to be their true selves. No character in this play except Lövborg is capable of this kind of love. Instead, we have the institution and ges-tures of love, even its pledge, which serve as means of deceit and self-deception, and the kind-hearted and erotic attitudes that still seem to partake of the essence of love.

Charitable love is displayed principally by Tesman's

two aunts, Juliana and Rina. They took their orphaned nephew into their home and gave him a university education. Now that Tesman is married and has been awarded his doctoral degree, they have put up the security for the debts he has incurred because of Hedda's luxurious tastes. Juliana devotedly nurses her sister Rina, who is close to death after a long illness. When Rina dies, she immediately makes plans to take in another "poor sick creature," who needs to be "looked after and cared for." In this case, however, we shall do well to draw a critical distinction between appearance and reality. While the gestures of unselfish love are obvious, its essence is lacking, or, rather, perverted. Love accepts the other as a person, because he is spirit or can be determined by spirit. Hence, love turns toward what is personal, valuable, and worthy of life in the other.

In Juliana Tesman this basic orientation of love is reversed. Instead of turning toward the personality of the other, she acts out of a long-standing habit of making people dependent on her in order to keep herself busy. Unselfishness is only a cover for self-negligence and self-negation. Thus, the other person is for her just a case or, to be more explicit, a case to be nursed. In contravention of the law of love, what Juliana's apparent altruism finds lovable is infirmity and invalidism, that is, frailty of personal character. It is not by accident that she ferrets out the infantile quality in the invalids she takes care of. It is not just from want of tact that she drives Hedda, whose pregnancy she recognizes at first sight, into utter despair by her constant allusions to her delicate condition. In her eyes the function of marriage is reduced to providing mankind with new nurslings.

The case of Tesman himself shows that Juliana's attitude toward people does not deny or try to eliminate physical infirmity and mental immaturity for the sake of the potential wholeness and perfectibility that can be glimpsed through their frailty and need for help. On the contrary, she accepts and fosters invalidism and narrowness. For only a person who is not entirely his own master can serve as a means of dispelling the emptiness and unfulfillment of her own existence by keeping her busy. This is a vicious circle in which one person falls victim to another. Juliana Tesman took charge of her nephew Jörgen when he was helpless, and she obviously did all she could to prevent his emancipation to self-determination. At the opening of the play Tesman has, it is true, assumed the social roles that, for society, usually signal man's maturity—profession and marriage. But Ibsen mercilessly reveals that he is incapable of realizing these forms of life or can only treat them as outlets for his infantilism.

Ibsen suggests from the first that Tesman is going to live in nursery conditions in "the villa of the late widow of Secretary Falk," the purchase of which Juliana has negotiated during the honeymoon and which she has helped him to furnish by mortgaging her annuity. The first act opens with only two characters on stage, Juliana and Tesman's old nurse Berta, now maid to the elderly aunts. Now that Tesman has returned, Juliana parts with Berta, making her promise to be a loyal servant in her nephew's household: "Jörgen simply must have you here in the house. He can't do without you. After all, you've looked after him all these years, ever since he was a little boy."

The audience soon sees that she is right. Tesman's stiffness, his dependency, and his need of support are revealed even in the set expressions with which he ends his sentences: "Eh?" "Think of that, Hedda!" "Think of that, Auntie Julia!" Tesman cannot realize himself in marriage. He is incapable of a loving relationship with Hedda because his capacity for love is fixed on the mother figure of his aunt. Only with her does he exchange loving gestures; only in talking to her does he use a pet name.

Tesman cannot free himself for self-understanding and self-realization because his character is irreversibly dominated by his past, inseparably bound to his background. Juliana points up his immature dependency by repeatedly referring to this young husband and doctor of philosophy as "my late brother's son." (She never mentions his mother, having taken over that role herself to fill the emptiness of her existence.) The future, in which the present is fulfilled, renewal of life, and regeneration are all foreign to Tesman's understanding. He wants to use the two vacant rooms in the house to enlarge his study, that is, as a storeroom for amassing tradition. In these rooms, however, Juliana, indulging her obsessive fancies, can already see her dear departed brother's grandchildren growing up, though she sees growth only as physical.

Lastly, it is Tesman's ill fate that he is unable to grow toward his self through his profession. The book he is writing deals with Brabantine crafts in the Middle Ages, a subject far removed in time and space. His honeymoon soon turned into a research journey, devoted to browsing endlessly through archives, making copies, sorting out and accumulating material. Professionally, then, he is also dedicated to preserving, restoring, and reconstructing what is dead. There is no indication that his restoration of the past could ever take on a meaningful, relevant vitality. Practiced in this way, his profession can never provide him with a subject or an activity in which he could actualize and realize himself.

Hedda keeps referring to Tesman as a "specialist," and she does not mean it as a compliment. The

description is both perceptive and critical. It limits
Tesman's adulthood and independence to the historical
dimensions to which for him the world and even his
own self have been reduced. It also indicates that his
thinking, feeling, and acting, insofar as they are not
connected with the mother-aunt figure, concentrate
exclusively on fact. Indeed, his whole being is rooted
in the prepersonal as well as the impersonal. Hence, he
is continually avoiding self-discovery and confrontation of the truth as defined as "object of eternal
approach" (to quote Sartre).

His aunt, who addresses him as "dear boy," and
facts, which have become history, give him no incen-
tive to break away from his locked-up self. Human
beings enter his life only as mediators of facts. Hedda,
being in his eyes an unalterable person, is not real to
him. Reifying her, he makes her into a decoration in
his new life. Embracing his aunt, he says: "Oh yes,
Auntie Julia. Yes, Hedda is really the most beautiful
part of it all." His renewed relationship with Lövborg,
whom he has not seen for a long time, rests on the
book Lövborg is preparing for publication. Nor does
his preoccupation with facts lead him back to the personal element reflected in them. Tesman's relation to
Lövborg acquires a purpose only after Lövborg is dead,
and then only through something material. When Lövborg's mode of being becomes part of history, Tesman
decides to devote all his time to sorting out his notes.

Hedda does not appear until the first act is fairly
well under way and Ibsen has revealed the human
inadequacies of Tesman and his aunt. It is her fate
to live at a time when mask play had lost its charm
and meaning. Her melancholy clear-sightedness recognizes that she belongs to an age when the traditional
forms of life have outlived themselves. ("The leaves—
they're so yellow and withered. . . . We're well into

September." . . . The villa of the late Secretary has a stale, dead smell "like flowers the morning after a night of dancing." . . . "I had danced myself tired. My time was running out.")

Hedda's language makes it clear that she does not subject human existence to ethical imperatives. She does not recognize moral decay but regrets the loss of vital exuberance and joy of living. But, unlike Tesman, she is painfully aware of the decadence of social conditions and personal relations and is not prepared to play any further role in them. By delaying her entrance, Ibsen intended to show, by means of the dialogue between Tesman and Juliana, that the position Hedda ought to occupy has been preempted by Juliana. By revealing the nature of Tesman and Juliana, who represent an obsolete, decadent society, Ibsen is implying that Hedda has some right on her side in her refusal to commit herself seriously to any person or any aim as a reaction to the degeneration of society. Juliana's example has exposed the mother role as destructive, while Tesman has made marriage and professional life seem denatured and sterile.

Hedda, however, suffers from the same inadequacies as Tesman and his aunt. She too has failed to achieve self-realization. The only difference is that her failure is not expressed in infantilism but in a critical split that separates action from thought. She has hidden behind social roles, although she is aware of their meaninglessness. Even self-deceit is beyond her. She does not believe she can play the role of wife successfully, and she does not try to. Not for one moment does she forget that she is playing a double game. On the contrary, she can exist only as long as she can turn every relationship into a game—something implying no responsibilities.

As the title of the play proves, she only agreed to

marry Tesman, after losing her money and finding that she was "beginning to be talked about," in order to remain Hedda Gabler, General Gabler's daughter. She degrades other people by making them a means of improving her own life, much as Tesman and Juliana do. The immorality and senselessness of her decision show that Hedda, too, is unhappily fixed in her background and in obsolete traditions that annul man's moral nature. Hedda is caught in the role of daughter, just as Tesman cannot free himself from the role of son. The portrait immortalizing her father—characteristically it shows him in full general's uniform—hangs sacrosanct above the sofa. Her actions if nothing else are oriented toward the father image. To her, the father represents social authority, always forcing her back into the situation of a child. In her marriage she plays the same kind of deceitful tricks on Tesman as she had played on her father. The fear of scandal constantly hanging over her stifles all her courage for open, declarative action. Also revealing is her identification of authority exclusively with men. She tries to take advantage of the helpless Tesman through deceit, but she confronts women with open defiance.

Her way of thinking also bears the military stamp of her general-father. Her otherwise incorruptible judgment seems to be ideologically obscured by an atavistic class consciousness. Hedda has an irresistible desire to make the people she comes in contact with feel déclassé. She pretends to mistake Juliana's new hat for the maid's. She deliberately downgrades her old schoolmate Thea Elvsted from a governess to a housekeeper. Since this desire is directed chiefly toward women, there is reason to suspect that she fundamentally classifies people by sex rather than social standing. But her desire to make men, too, look contemptible shows that Hedda is really interested in effecting a more basic degradation. Her aim is abasement, which scornfully exposes the emptiness of man when he is deprived of the roles he plays.

In any case, Hedda's fate, because of her fixation on her father, is that of being a woman with a masculine attitude to the world. This forces her into a position that the social system precludes. If she still wants to satisfy her lust for power, she will have to think of new expedients. She finds one in her marriage to Tesman. This marriage gives her the social position in which she can exercise power over people. Here we glimpse another confusing ambivalence in Hedda, which reveals that her class consciousness and her desire to degrade others do not stem solely from the distant past but also from deep-lying sources. As usual, Hedda holds on to a traditional form of life but skillfully falsifies it and makes it serve her exceptional ego.

Her compulsion to dominate others is inseparably linked with an unconquerable fear of exposing herself and committing herself irrevocably to a relationship. This defensiveness reveals the other side of her arrogance. Although they take different directions, both are manifestations of her self-evasion. This tendency to protect herself also leads her to play a double game. By regularizing her position, her marriage to Tesman, whom she does not recognize even as a husband, enables her to pursue her relationships with other men as mere episodic games.

Clearly, Hedda understands the rotation system. Nothing finite must be given the status of finitude because she realizes its futility. But neither may her self commit itself, in any human constellation, to finality and self-awareness. She sees life as a journey; every situation is relativized to a "stage." Luxury of all kinds must be provided to amuse her and gratify her imperious desires. While Tesman mistakes the house for a library, Hedda wants to turn it into a salon in order to bring in the outside world to help her pass the time. Tesman is fortunate enough never to possess time; his unimportant occupations have consumed it in advance. To Hedda, though, time stretches ahead empty and desolate. She has to make desperate efforts to kill it.

But Hedda has fostered her aversion to knowledge too well; she has too much acuity to succeed in escaping from herself. Melancholy and its sister, boredom, catch up with her. Kierkegaard perceptively called melancholy "hysteria of the spirit." In melancholy the spirit announces its imminent breakthrough. In the spirit the self is grounded—self in the sense of the capacity to seize and realize oneself in freely taken decision. To avoid facing the challenge of the spirit, which presses for self-understanding and self-realization, one escapes into melancholy, the guilty weakness of "not willing deeply and sincerely," to quote Kierkegaard again. But melancholy, unlike activity, cannot smother confrontation of the self in trivialities. It forces those it afflicts into the obfuscating experience of finding the self and the world branded as worthless.

Melancholy lurks behind the majestic, sovereign gesture with which Hedda manipulates other people's lives for her own amusement, whether she is playing a humiliating game or acting in dead seriousness. We read it in the tired expression to which her autocratic attitudes so easily give way and in the defensive gesture with which she tries to ward off the ugly and the absurd: "Please spare me from anything ugly. . . . Oh, I shall die of it! I simply can't stand it! . . . Everything! All this absurdity!" This shows how melancholy is succeeded by the uncreative desolation of boredom to which Hedda falls victim. She recognizes it herself: "I often think there's only one thing in this world I'm fitted for—boring myself to death!" Boredom, like melancholy, abrogates creation. In its undertow life turns into nonbeing, weary of itself and of the world as being absurd, ugly, worthless.

While Tesman's existence aims solely at overcoming this crisis, Hedda's existence is inevitably drawn into it. In addition to the above-mentioned factors, her pregnancy must be especially distressing to her because it represents a hateful perpetuation of life. But the sudden, catastrophic eruption of the crisis is precipitated by Lövborg's return to the Norwegian capital after a self-imposed exile in the north.

He is accompanied by Thea Elvsted, née Rying, an "old flame" of Tesman's and a school friend of Hedda's. Thea moved north when she married a provincial official, whom she does not love and who exploits her. Lövborg himself, a boyhood friend of Tesman's and once a passionate admirer of Hedda, is as entangled with the Tesmans by the strings of fate as Thea is. Lövborg is the only one who rejects compromise and thinks and acts radically, who wills the truth "deeply and sincerely" and strives with absolute seriousness for self-realization. And so catastrophe befalls him, and he drags others down with him. He is inevitably forced to break with society, which stifles the self in spiritual infantilism and false morality. He gives up an academic career promising a brilliant future. His absolutism, finding no creative outlet, turns to dissolute living. Truth can only manifest itself in the negation of everything that exists and has validity. Hedda belongs to him by virtue of her nature. She is as homeless in society as he is. But in her invincible fear of self-revelation and self-exposure she is ultimately not equal to the extremeness of his love, which demands total commitment and irrevocability. "When the game threatened to become serious," she withdrew from his love.

Hedda tries to conform, but the cost of her effort is a brooding reserve. Lövborg, however, draws a decisive and drastic conclusion: he has the courage to drop out of society. He disappears for several years and is written off as a drifter. The chaotic element in him begins to show itself. Since normality desolates the self and makes it impossible to find or experience truth, he abandons himself to abnormality, breaking down all barriers, seeking, beyond all fixations, direct, exciting certainty of existence, unrestricted freedom, and undistorted communication with reality. He seeks the degradations in which the nakedness of the self is revealed. He repudiates his former life and reverses its course.

Lövborg goes through a phase of dissolution, apparently destroying his life. But it seems that the cosmos of society is renewed by this chaotic destruction. After a short time he regains his social position in the Elvsted household. Characteristically, he does this by becoming a tutor, for his existence is based on education as well as realization, on his pedagogical will to perfect, to open up and to realize potentialities. And when a loving understanding quickly develops between him and Thea, he seems to be succeeding in recapturing what he is in search of. There are indeed several indications that Thea, who dares to implement her will "seriously, absolutely, and openly," represents to Lövborg a new Hedda who brings the fulfillment the real Hedda did not. Thea willingly accepts the role of "comrade," which Hedda had refused. In this way she gains "some sort of power over him," which is just what Hedda yearned to do.

Thea encourages Lövborg to make a fresh start and finally turns his firmness of purpose to creative ends. He publishes one book and has another in manuscript. The first one traces the development of civilization up to the present day. The second, a sequel, deals with the cultural forces of the future and sketches future cultural developments. Of course, these works and Tesman's manuscript are mutually antagonistic. Lövborg's ability to make his thought and actions consistent contrasts with Tesman's approach. Lövborg takes off from the present to arrive at the future. From self-education he has progressed to open, utopian pedagogy. His plans reflect faith in the future and see life as a process, the very opposite of Tesman's infantile, backward-looking stance. He always has realization and accomplishment in mind. And while Tesman's work deals with an aspect of culture dominated by traditional forms that had become rigid—with crafts that serve domestic purposes—the subject of Lövborg's books is culture itself, the medium through which man learns to interpret himself as spirit, to fulfill himself as a human being for the first time.

Lövborg's book is very well received, and he returns to the capital. He wants to win a real position for himself and competes with Tesman for the university chair. Thea, afraid that he may fall back into his old profligate ways, leaves her family to its fate and, without his knowledge, follows him. In the meantime, Hedda, seeking distraction from the boredom of her marriage and from her spiritual emptiness, has drifted into a flirtation with Judge Brack in which they treat each other as commodities but which has the advantage of not requiring any personal, social, or moral commitment. With the return of Lövborg, however, her drawing room becomes the scene of an exciting game in which the stakes are life and death. Hedda is fascinated by the imminent competition, although it may mean financial disaster for her. While Lövborg simply wants to bring things out into the open, Hedda is bent on revelations. She knows that Tesman will lose the competition, in which social position counts for nothing. It will show that social status is only a distorted—possibly even a reversed—reflection of human status.

Now Hedda's dark, elemental side becomes visible. Having seen through the depersonalizing effect of moral and social norms, she must strive for freedom, as Lövborg passionately desires it and as Thea seems to want it. But freedom requires her "seriously and finally" to choose her self. She evades this by trying to be free at somebody else's expense, as Camus said. Incapable of being "her own master," she presumes to master others. It is this that makes the kind of freedom she takes for autonomy so destructive.

Hedda makes herself the scourge of other people. To acquire the freedom she wants, to "hold a human fate in her power," she is compelled to degrade others, to show them the worthlessness of their existence and the emptiness of their forms of life and action. She forces the others into declaring moral bankruptcy and admitting truths that, if they face up to them, must inevitably drive them into despair and self-contempt. Hedda's aim must always be to degrade those around her, because their contemptibility excuses the human inadequacy of the general's daughter and her insistence on the past. In other words, she continues to cling to her atavistic role only in order to use others as a means of escaping from herself and lagging behind the truth of personality, which condemns her to stagnation and imprisons her in melancholy.

Hedda makes an example of Thea. Thea's "timid, questioning look" and her first fear-distorted words tell Hedda that the sustenance of her relationship with Lövborg is not mutual dedication to love and affirmation of it. On her part Thea degrades her relation to

Lövborg into a means of self-affirmation. With the talent for detecting imperfections that her melancholy inspires, Hedda has quickly sensed that Thea lacks the readiness to trust "absolutely and unreservedly" that Lövborg attributes to her. Complete trust would mean encouraging Lövborg to develop his self, because trust implies the will to desire truth. Trust overcomes inadequacy and self-betrayal, because it can perceive the truth, which by its very essence belongs to the future, within the imperfection of present reality.

Thea, however, does not accept Lövborg for the sake of the truth to which he might perfect himself: she does not accept him for his sake but for her own. To her, the relationship is no more than a way of making something of her life. It is characteristic of Thea that her life does not grow toward its innate meaning but that she tries to find in her life a meaning that is not properly hers. Like Juliana, she desperately needs someone to live for. Juliana is not the only one who is driven to stay on the path she has chosen lest her life spin off into the void or she be compelled to face new realities. For the same reason, Thea reacts to Lövborg's return, which is prompted by an upsurge of independence, and to his radical new departure with "deadly fear." Fear arises when the assumed meaning dissolves, revealing existential nothingness. Under these circumstances it is easy enough for Hedda, with a diffidently cowardly craftiness, to lead Thea and Lövborg into a crisis of trust. Thea responds with despair; Lövborg, with pathos: "Thanks for the truth. Long may it live!"

Ibsen himself would probably have turned this toast to truth into a question. Will the truth "finally and definitively" win out in at least two people? As the ending of the play shows, Thea again manages to evade the truth, which for Ibsen means *to be true*. Lövborg's case is more complicated. All attempts to recover meaning—attempts that men undertake only to cover up their despair by a lie—turn into absurdity. Lövborg therefore strives to return to unruly intransigence. He longs to be what he truly is behind all his roles, behind the social animal, even behind individuality, which has shown itself to be a false development.

The frenzy of life is supposed to fill the vacuum. The festivities at Judge Brack's house, which show every sign of turning into a bacchanalia, seem to offer an opportunity for such fulfillment. Hedda's imagination paints a Lövborg "flushed and fearless, with vine leaves in his hair." Here, the Dionysian element clearly enters, as so often occurs when emancipation of the spirit founders. The exuberance of existence, the spring of life, seem to be recaptured. This, too, is a way—indeed, the most radical way—of "making a fresh start." But, of course, this attempt also ends in disenchantment and disgust when Lövborg falls victim not to the maenads but to Diana, a notorious prostitute, and when his excesses call up not primeval forces but the police. The bacchanalia is quickly reduced to a night out with the boys.

Now it is the turn of Dionysus's quieter brother, Death. A longing for death seems to have been awakened in Lövborg. Even Hedda no longer wants to persuade him to make a fresh start. She wants to arouse his courage for nonexistence rather than for existence. Truth does not reside in beginnings but at the point at which life comes to an end, where all apparent meaning is shattered. The only action Hedda still recognizes and upholds as a free, courageous *act* is suicide, which turns against all action and in which action annuls itself. Suicide is indeed the only act in which she recognizes the quality of necessity, the only one that seems to her to derive logically from Lövborg's nature. To choose death means "to do what had to be done."

She therefore encourages Lövborg's need to die. She hands him the pistol with which she had playfully threatened Brack, her suitor for the time being, in order to satisfy her destructive desire for truth and find out whether his mask of flippant self-assurance will not be contorted into the grimace of self-abandoned fear when it is confronted by the irrevocable. And she consigns Lövborg's manuscript, which has fallen into her hands, to the flames. Hedda's hatred turns against this manuscript, which is repeatedly referred to as Thea's and Lövborg's child. She will not allow truth to be overturned. Life is seemingly resanctified through work, but this is man's cheapest and most common relief in his flight from self-awareness. Instead of being inexorably led back to his own self, man is always in danger of being diverted into supposedly meaningful tasks and into relationships with his fellowman, whom he supposedly accepts for the sake of his personality. Through work humanity is given a promise of rebirth; culture is promised a future.

And now Lövborg is at the point of allowing not truth but self-evasion, decked out in lies, to motivate his action and thought. So Hedda euphorically awaits the suicide that she has tried to lead Lövborg to. Life itself now seems the enemy of truth. To satisfy man's dim urge for survival, life must constantly supply him with fresh motivations that seem to justify his existence. In death man fulfills his essential being. Hedda believes that Lövborg will reestablish his self through death. He will regain the freedom and courage that make him an autonomous master of himself. Triumphing over the truth-evading or melancholy sin of failing to will seriousness and finality, he will be transfigured into "beauty," in which truth manifests itself.

But Ibsen mercilessly reveals this euphoric expectation as Hedda's last illusion and diversion for evading her own truth. Shot by Diana, the prostitute, Lövborg dies in ignominious and repulsive circumstances. Diana is mysteriously linked with Hedda. She too has red hair. Thea, to her embarrassment, confuses the two in talking about an obscure liaison of Lövborg's. Thus, Diana is a manifestation of Hedda; she represents the Hedda who has the courage openly to refute social morality and put an end to an unessential life, thus fulfilling the destiny her name implies. From Hedda, who uses her own morality for self-deception and exploitation instead of for spiritual purification and humanization, Lövborg turned to Diana, who at least takes her contempt for morality seriously.

Yet this crude and vulgar death, so out of keeping with Lövborg's social position, which so brutally challenges Hedda's dishonest fantasy of a "beautiful" corpse, still has the power to spread truth. Tesman and Thea are forever lost to self-realization. Lövborg's death provides them with a new occupation, with a possibility of blocking even their future self-awareness. Their tireless efforts will piece together the scattered notes of Lövborg's manuscript, which his death has already refuted. With self-deluding energy they will restore the past that has already become meaningless. These two, so similar in their inadequacies, will now make a couple, if only in the service of a thing. The relationship that society, with its hostility to truth, imposed upon Hedda and Tesman, Lövborg and Thea, reversed their natural affinities.

In choosing death, Hedda, too, finally declares her allegiance to Lövborg—and not only because she will henceforward be at the mercy of Brack because he has recognized the pistol that kills Lövborg as hers. Hedda stops playing her eternal games and decides upon the irrevocable. The game is over, or, rather, it has become serious. After playing a wild dance on the piano, Hedda shoots herself through the temple. Once again we see how close Dionysian self-dissolution is to death. Obviously, Hedda's death is the logical end of an existence that has not fought through to its self and now demands self-liberation; but it is at least a logical end.

The curtain falls on an exclamation by Brack: "People just don't do such things!" This sentence recurs as a leitmotif throughout the play. Hedda herself, who separated action and thought and suppressed self-recognition because of her fear of scandal, sometimes says it. Thus, her suicide proves how far she has outdistanced Brack in the end.

The Master Builder

With this "drama in three acts" Ibsen begins the group of late works that center on the theme the German poet and essayist Gottfried Benn formulated as "aging as a problem for the artist." Ibsen himself pointed to a continuous line leading from *The Master Builder* to the "dramatic epilogue," *When We Dead Awaken*. The former play is pervaded by the sunlight of two late summer days, September 19 and 20, days of an Indian summer that inexorably leads the year into autumn.

Halvard Solness, "a man in the prime of life," typifies dividedness. His whole being is frustrated by the "halfness" his first name suggests. He has a strong desire to "rise high," but an unconquerable "dizziness" drags him down into anxiety and fear and prevents him from living self-confidently—"lighthearted and free." He unscrupulously pursues his own interests, but his delicate conscience forces him to see his ambitions in the light of universal ethical standards. Furthermore, he is torn between technology and magic, solipsism and visions of unity, unscrupulous exploitation and missionary projects. These contradictions point to a fragmented self.

Solness, like many of Ibsen's grandly conceived power seekers and craftsmen, wants the pyramid of his life to tower as high as possible. But this striving has nothing of the fundamental seriousness that goes into one's making oneself into the personality one wants to be. It is rather an unrestrained desire to raise the self to absolute mastery. Solness has no regard for his true self, and one can only develop one's true self by deliberately choosing to do so. He follows his natural bent, which resists ethical imperatives.

Solness does not hide this lack of self-emancipation: "I can't do anything else, you see. I am the way I am. And I can't remake myself." As the text suggests, he counts on *tyche* (luck) to help him to climb high, as indeed it does. Starting as a "poor country boy," he succeeds, through his marriage to Aline, in rising quickly to a high social position. But since he is a dilettante in his profession as well as in life—he is a failed architect—he must again rely on the help of circumstances to "climb to the top" as a master builder. The house that Aline inherited from her family had to be gotten rid of so that its spacious garden could be divided into building lots, thus giving free scope to his desire to build. (It is already clear that Solness can only base the edifice of his life on ruins whose *genius loci* has lost its power.)

Solness does not intervene in reality with the idea of extending or reshaping it. He is committed to a principle that tends to stray into the "impossible" and the demonic—imagination. The nucleus around which his magical ideas crystallize is a crack in the chimney. His wish that this defect may cause a fire is so pressing that he cannot bring himself to repair it. If his self were whole in an evil sense, he would bring himself to set fire to the house, but he contents himself with "wishing . . . desiring . . . willing." And when we look more closely, the Master Builder's powers of making things happen are not as effective as his confession would indicate. Since neither mere willing nor blind desire leads to action, he is forced back to the passive form of endeavor: mere wishing. *Desiring* and *willing* are only inadequate descriptions of a wish that is experienced as something "persistent" and "unshakable."

Solness populates the earth with demonic "helpers and servers, good devils and bad devils." In them return, as impersonal powers, all the forces that he has failed to integrate in his self, which lacks what Kierkegaard called "the binding force of personality." His wishing is so powerful that it seems to force the "helpers" into his service. A ruinous fire breaks out—though in a clothes closet, so that he is not even personally guilty. But his self is so diffuse, slips so easily into the impersonal and the prepersonal, that when things happen just as he wants them to happen he inevitably thinks this is his own doing. While Solness steadily rises to become the most famous master builder in the whole region, his wishful magic (which, as Kierkegaard says, brings personal life to a halt) forces him into a troll-like isolation. Both his little sons (twin babies only a few weeks old) die from complications caused by the fire.

Aline, not equipped for individuality, married to a man who does not bind others, finally withdraws into the past that Solness has ruined for her without freeing her from it. Her mind and feelings are obsessed by the family possessions she lost in the fire. Her life drifts back to the stiff figures of her childhood—the dolls with whom she "went on living together" and whom she "carried under her heart like unborn children." Never has Ibsen depicted infantile behavior more outspokenly. In her unproductive reliving and reexperiencing of the past she has no access to people of the present. Whenever she has to have anything to do with them, she withdraws into "duty," invariably formalizing and depersonalizing her relationship to others. Ibsen characterizes her in this leitmotif: "After all, that's my duty."

So far as Solness is concerned, it seems that "art has become impossible without diabolical help," to quote Thomas Mann. The law that splits his existence is already becoming plain. As one side of his self realizes itself, another falls into atavism. Self-liberation is achieved only at the cost of confusion. But Solness is not yet aware of this law. His self has no clear boundary line against the world of intermediate beings. He interprets inner developments as outer effects, and therefore takes the disintegration and self-mutilation of which he has become guilty as a sacrifice forced upon him. He suspects that God put at his service the "helpers," who obviously had something to do with the fire and who are responsible for his isolation, in order to commit him more firmly to his traditional occupation—building churches to God's greater glory.

Characteristically, Solness conceives God as a super-troll, a Master of Kobolds. He addresses him as "Mighty One," reducing him to a being who has power over others. "To be a free master builder," he breaks away from God. Here Ibsen points to a new contradiction in Solness's existence. His break with God and his proclamation of man as a personality that is its own master corresponds to his regression into the archaic, the preindividual. (He finds the courage to reject God after having built a tower for the church in Lysanger.

For the first time in his life he overcomes his dizziness and himself carries the wreath up to the top of the scaffolding.)

Thus, Solness has raised the pyramid of his existence high into the air—although it rests on a troll. And now he falls into a further contradiction. This man, who has dissociated himself from human communion, might have been inspired by the program of Ibsen's "third empire." He wants in future to build houses for human beings, "homes where a father and a mother and a whole troop of children could live in the secure, joyful feeling that just to exist in this world is heavenly good fortune." Once again Ibsen reveals the fatal connection between vanguardism and primitivism.

Judging by outward appearances, Solness continues his rise. He employs his former teacher, Brovik, now old and mortally ill, and the latter's ambitious son Ragnar. (Brovik is responsible for the calculation of "bearing capacities"—which is suggestive enough.) Ragnar wants to make himself independent, and to design buildings of his own that would make Solness look old-fashioned. To chain this independent-minded young man to him, the Master Builder succeeds in getting Ragnar's fiancée Kaja to fall in love with him and engages her as a bookkeeper. Ibsen is telling the audience that Solness, by acquiring influence over other people's lives, gets the benefit of such tendencies as he has failed to integrate in his own self: Kaja's capacity for love, Ragnar's striving for self-realization, Brovik's professional competence.

But even in his rugged egoism Solness can only *appear* to be free and whole. He cannot free himself from traditional ethics, which he has evaded but not revalued, or from the traditional concept of personality, which he has ignored but not reshaped. The "delicate conscience," which plagues him constantly, renews the hold of the objective values, which he wanted to break away from. The guilt feelings that torment him make him blame himself for wrongs that seem beyond his responsibility.

And yet it looks as if Solness were not so much at variance with himself as threatened by the outside world. He is mistrustful; he feels that he is the object of suspicion. Above all, he fears—and there is a deeper significance in this—that he is suspected of madness. And he knows that he is a prey to desire for revenge. But these worries are reflections of his doubt in his own self, which he projects onto other people.

Solness objectifies the disintegration of inner forces not only in his helpers but also in his adversaries. The younger generation is the most serious threat to his self-assurance because he is sure that it seeks revenge and will exact inexorable retribution. This is understandable, for only "with youth" can one hold one's own "against youth." Thus, unlived life takes its revenge on Solness. The youthful capacity for absolute self-fulfillment, which he has never realized, now puts the man (or rather his manliness) in question. We remember the scene in which Peer Gynt is pronounced guilty of deeds left undone and recognize how boldly Ibsen, in his old age, embodied his own emotions in characters, characters who possess a validity of their own.

Solness is at a turning point in life, like the one that finds the Wangels in *The Lady from the Sea* and the Allmers in *Little Eyolf* struggling toward "transformation." This is the moment when the drama can be set in motion, because now the crisis, which has been threatening for many years, flares up. At the beginning of the first act Ibsen exposes the symptoms that announce its eruption. Although apparently "healthy and strong," Solness seems to be creatively exhausted.

He has made no sketches for a building commissioned long ago. In the first scene he meets with his three assistants—a split character among broken ones.

Solness can no longer hide his fears and lassitude. It is an effort to him to keep up the pretense of being in love with Kaja. He is tired of deceptions. The atmosphere is growing oppressive. A double game is being played everywhere, carried out by exchanges of ambiguous or whispered words, suppressed emotions, retracted confessions. Nobody acts spontaneously or appears in the shape that would truly reflect his being.

It is, however, uncertain whether the crisis denotes renewal or dissolution. Solness is building a new house into which he plans to move with Aline. Built on the site of the fire, its tower rising proudly into the air, it is almost ready for the roof-raising celebration. Solness seems to want to initiate a new era. He wants to stop wavering between the untranscended past and the future that he will have attained and is determined to mediate between the two (as he mediated between the two phases of his architectural aspirations). He builds the edifice of his life on the past instead of soaring above it to the heights.

Yet Solness is so unsuccessful in shaking off the spell of the past that for the first time he feels compelled to speak about it, in a conversation with Dr. Herdal, his family doctor. But Herdal (who offers plenty of evidence of his lack of understanding) cannot straighten out the tangled skein of the past. Even in dreams, his scientific mind could never conceive the atavism to which Solness is enslaved. The past, now inescapable, comes forward in the guise of "biological friendliness" (to use Thomas Mann's phrase) in the person of youth, representing seduction. In the words of the stage directions, "Hilda Wangel enters."

Hilda is in her early twenties. It is ten years to the

day since she enthusiastically waved to Solness when he fastened the wreath to the top of the tower at Lysanger. She was then a girl of twelve or thirteen, fascinated by a man who "can climb as high as he has built." Hilda's memory is much more accurate than Solness dares to remember. She vividly recalls that after the roof-raising celebration he took her in his arms, kissed her "many times," and promised to come back on the tenth anniversary of September 19 and present her with a kingdom called Orangia. Hilda has to help Solness to recall this promise. He has forgotten it and resists her reminiscence with strong disclaimers. It makes little difference whether all this actually happened as Hilda's memory recalls it, indeed whether it actually happened at all. Her memory, reaching down into the depths of time, retains something that holds its own against all reality—the troll-like wishing and passive desiring of Solness.

In a brilliant essay the German dramatist Frank Wedekind interpreted *The Master Builder* as Ibsen's confrontation of his own dramatic ambitions in a superficially individualized personification and pointed out the masculine traits in Hilda's character. While subscribing to this, we would interpret it slightly differently. Hilda is an incarnation of Solness's extravagant urge to strive upward. In her, however, the desire is absolute and not hampered by a "dizzy conscience" or earthward-dragging guilt feelings. She is the sort of woman a troll might dream up in his own image. Of course, this masculine tendency does not prevent Hilda from being totally committed to erotic allurement. (She, too, is given to fantasies, as we see from her confession that she enjoys the falling sensation she experiences in dreams.)

If one judges by her way of life, behavior, and clothes, Hilda is definitely emancipated. She has left her father for good and set out "without a suitcase" to demand her kingdom. But either appearances are deceptive or we must eliminate from the term "emancipation" all idea of progress in time toward self-realization. Clearly, Hilda, like many of Ibsen's characters, is rooted in an adolescent experience to such an extent that she is deceived into interpreting her pleasure in the past as a desire for a fulfilling future. (Of course, Solness too is similarly characterized, in that his burning desire makes sense only to an adolescent.) Hilda sees the passage of time as fairy-tale heroes do; as a return of propitious moments when wishes are fulfilled, provided one is in the right place at the right time. For her the intervening years have been such a passage of time.

In Hilda, Ibsen makes a delightful and successful departure from his basic dramatic technique and introduces a feminine character in search of the hero: Hilda is clearly determined to arouse in Solness the courage to regain the height he once climbed to in a moment of troll-like recklessness. (In the imagery of the play, she wants to make him carry the wreath up to the tower of the new building.) Heroes, it seems, are no longer born of self-transcendence and the discovery of a demonic freedom in the breast but out of regression and fascinating enticement. Vanguardism is finally revealed as regression. Hilda explicitly wants to commit the Master Builder to the atavistic Viking ethos. The word "exciting" denotes the highest value she recognizes. To bring Solness to his full height again, she must get rid of his conscience and his sense of guilt.

Thus, the inner form of the play is a series of delaying actions. In the process of implementing her unconditional demand, Hilda finds herself in a situation in which she prompts a recapitulation of the prehistory.

(For purposes of simplification I have dealt with this first.) As she explores Aline's past, she even has momentary qualms of conscience. She apparently stimulates the Master Builder to truth and self-loyalty, reconciles him with his inmost will, and liberates him to himself. Little by little she frees him from all the people to whom he was tied: from Ragnar, whom he releases to independence; from Kaja, whom he had been using as an instrument of "self-punishment" because she gave Aline reason to suspect him of unfaithfulness; and from his wife, to whom he was "chained as if to a corpse." (Brovik, tortured by disappointment in his son, dies of a stroke before the news of Ragnar's independence reaches him.) But just as in this play the past wears the mask of the future, regression into the archaic wears the grimace of progress toward morality. For while Hilda emancipates Solness from his divided self and lures him out of his "halfness," the goal of the process she sets in motion is not a self that will develop itself in life but a fraudulent youth, a transformation back into pure troll.

The prehistory is recounted not chronologically but episodically, with subtle interlocking and overlapping, following a law designed to make us increasingly aware of the obscurely rooted, extravagant element in Solness. The account of his wrestling with God comes at the end, late in the third act, so that the climb he undertakes immediately afterward is seen in its light. First, however, comes a piece of stage business with the wreath. It is Ragnar who hands it to the Master Builder. The younger generation foretells his end, for this wreath points to death, not to a renewal of life. Urged on by Hilda, Solness tries once more to scale the heights. He climbs to the top but is overcome by dizziness and falls to his death.

John Gabriel Borkman

John Gabriel Borkman, prophetic herald of an industrial era, has dark origins. From his father, a miner, he has a nocturnal heritage; his maternal background is obscure and shadowy. This titan of the dawning industrial age seems to derive his elemental powers from Mother Earth. Without doubt he has some kinship with the realms of nature and earth.

Borkman's existence is held by the spell of a childhood experience. His father would sometimes take him down the mines with him, and he has been fascinated ever since by the infinite treasures in their depths. "The imprisoned millions" called to him to free them. The "singing" and "ringing" of the metal, longing to be broken out and liberated, bewitched him. The fascination of the treasures lying buried in the earth was transmuted into a music that would not let him go. Now an old man, he still loves music "rich in evocative gestures of incantation" (to use Thomas Mann's phrase) although he now hears in it both the resonant ring of the metal and the death song of the "Danse Macabre." The two are indistinguishably blended, just as in the mine the ore gleams and the grave yawns.

152

Borkman's relation to the world, then, is based on allurement and seduction. The fascinating ring of metal resounds throughout the play, from the first act to the last. Once, as John Gabriel rose rapidly, with the undeviating sureness of the sleepwalker, to power and riches, it was echoed in the fine ring of the name Borkman, a name that suggests his origin—the dark abyss of the miner's world.

The fatal split in Borkman's nature comes from his bondage to the world of the past. This power-hungry man with the bearing of a king, spellbound by the primeval, has glorious dreams, which, if realized, would broaden civilization and produce progress and a democratic mass society. His utopian vision foresees gigantic industrial landscapes reaching to the horizon and a network of shipping lines crisscrossing the oceans, carrying worldwide trade beyond continental limits. He prophesies the exploitation of mineral resources to bring "light and warmth to thousands of huts and homes" and "prosperity to thousands and thousands of people." But these ambitious plans, which would mean emancipating man from nature, have not overcome the troll-like element in Borkman. On the contrary, his visions are an expression of this element, which he cannot shake off. The omnipotence and fraudulence of his wishful fancies, which, like children's dreams, impose their own law on reality, already show that Borkman's sense of self is a magical one and that he lacks seriousness toward reality and mastery of life.

Another contradiction is evident in Borkman's conduct. This lordly man, who commands such power and wishes to free thousands of people from the tribulations of nature, is unfree at the core, which directs his thoughts and actions. He is possessed by an indomitable urge"; he has "no choice." As he says himself, "I couldn't act any differently because I was the man I am, because I was John Gabriel Borkman." His desire for power, which is insatiable, spurs him to Promethean and creative demonstrations and efforts of will, carries him away in visions of revolutionary utopias. But mighty and far-reaching as his will is, he is totally unfree. He has no ethos; he is dominated by mere drive.

This revolutionary character appears in the hide of a troll; this speculative mind degenerates into a speculator. Borkman, the great exploiter, exploits human beings as well as everything else. To him, the life of the "spirits," which pay homage to him from the depths of the earth, seems richer in reality than human life. The treasures imprisoned in the mines inspire him to poetic improvisations. He breathes life into them, gives them "shape and voice," feels drawn by their "luring arms." Finally, this Peer Gynt of the industrial age, who is otherwise opposed to all "emotional nonsense," works himself up to an excited declaration of love: "I love you, you treasures clamoring for life, with all your shining train of power and glory. I love you, love you, love you!"

But Borkman's actions are subject to the law of demonic compensation. The love he gives the spirits in the depths is that which he withholds from human beings. He destroys in those nearest to him the life force that he wants to awaken in the metals. The prosperity he wants to bring to thousands of people in the future will be attained at the expense of those now living. Borkman, whose sense of reality is weak, sacrifices what is at hand (including the people closest to him) to a vaguely visualized world of the past and an imaginatively anticipated future.

To obtain the bank directorship he wants, Borkman relinquishes to Hinkel, a lawyer and his rival in business and love, what is "then and afterwards—long, long after . . . the dearest thing in the world" to him— Ella Rentheim. He himself, "obeying inexorable necessity," marries Ella's twin sister, Gunhild. Ella, however, refuses to marry Hinkel. Borkman, rising higher and higher, "half way up to the beckoning heights," embarks on great ventures. To found big corporations in order to lead the earth into the age of technology, he embezzles bank deposits. But torn by dark compulsions and regal arrogance and enslaved to the omnipotence of magic or technology, Borkman fails to become his own master and perishes from halfheartedness.

He sins against the basic principle of all action, the principle that the whole man must move at once; and this causes his fall. His enterprises oscillate between deeds and misdeeds, and this ambivalence can be traced back to their very source—Borkman himself. He admits that he doubts even when he believes, for in addition to his troll-like lust for power he also possesses a conscience. Instead of reconciling the two, he divorces his conscience from his actions. "With total frankness," he informs Hinkel of his frauds. (Obviously, his relation to other people wavers between deceitfulness and blind trust.) This divorcing of conscience and actions, this inability to be responsible to himself, turns out to be his ruin. Hinkel, who blames Borkman for Ella's refusal to marry him, reports his offenses to the authorities. Borkman, now bankrupt, is sentenced to eight years in prison.

The play opens on a winter evening sixteen years after "that dreadful event." Its setting is the Rentheim estate, just outside Oslo, which Ella turned over to the ruined Borkmans. Here Gunhild watches the years go by in a drawing room "furnished with old-fashioned, faded splendor." Erhart, the son of Borkman and

Gunhild, is a student in Oslo, but he visits his mother "for a little while" every evening. Upstairs, in what used to be the great hall, the ruined Borkman has dragged out his life ever since his release from prison. Since shame fell upon the family, Gunhild and Borkman have never looked one another in the eye or exchanged a word. Ella, who lives on the west coast of Norway for the sake of its milder climate, has no contact with them. Borkman had not touched her fortune, and immediately after his bankruptcy she took Erhart to live with her. Since Gunhild demanded the return of her son, Ella has not visited her tenants.

Living in an unreal world of faded splendor, condemned to ineffectuality, Borkman has given himself over to wishes, delusions, and dreams. Gunhild, too, wanting only to purge her family of shame, stifles reality in fantasies. Their minds are set on vindication. Imprisoned in a dream of the past, they have both stopped trying to influence reality. Both of them mistake their past for the future, inasmuch as any future remains to them. They are living the delusion that reality, weightlessly gliding like reality in dreams, will follow the scenario dictated by their wishes. This can be seen in the following lines:

> GUNHILD: Let it come about as best it can. All I know is that it must and will happen some day.

> BORKMAN: When the hour of my vindication comes . . . when it strikes for me. . . .

Once again Ibsen has taken on something that is not exactly a task for a dramatist. He is dealing with characters whose power of decision is broken, who have turned from action to dreams, and who seek to avoid self-searching not merely through masks, like most of

Ibsen's other characters, but through total silence. To get these people engaged in dramatic action or even in dialogue takes skill. Once again it is too late to create and conclude a human destiny; once again the characters can do no more than accept an existence botched by false pretensions. The decisive figure—the one who brings about decisions—is Ella Rentheim. The ill health from which she has suffered ever since the emotional shock of Borkman's betrayal makes it unlikely that she will survive the winter that has just begun. She appears unexpectedly to win back Erhart (whom she loves "as much as she can love anyone now") from Gunhild and to get Borkman to allow her to adopt him.

Ella obeys a law different from those of Gunhild and Borkman. Facing death and aware of its inevitability, she wills immediately and decisively. She forces the Borkmans to see time as something in which movement occurs; she brings about or hastens decisions and confrontations. At the end of the first act she prompts Erhart to come into the room—"out of hiding," as Gunhild says—and at the end of Act III she calls upon him to declare himself master of his fate. She also calls the others to account, especially Borkman, and engages them in dialogue. She breaks up the parallel arrangement of the characters, which could never become dramatic, and makes them confront each other through dialogue, at least for the duration of the play (which coincides with the time it takes to perform it).

Nevertheless, Ibsen did not use Ella just to graft a soliloquizing self on to the play. Her arrival at the house is abundantly and skillfully motivated. Because, like the others, she must learn to renounce illusions, she, too, is a victim of the dramatic events. And although her presence on the stage makes the whole play possible, Ibsen also had to invent other methods of presenting in visual terms lives that have withdrawn deep within themselves. Every stage detail, from the tarnished splendor of the rooms to the curtained windows, every idiosyncrasy, from Ella's "good eyes" to Gunhild's constant chilliness, serves the purpose of dramatic revelation. Ibsen constantly had to think up visible correlatives for inner happenings. First, he invented the figure of Foldal, a government clerk and a failed writer, to bring out characteristics, tendencies, and potentialities that lie hidden in Borkman. He did not hesitate to let his characters use back doors, so to speak, and overhear conversations which prompt answers and rebuttals.

The audience is not likely to object to these tricks, for it is soon captivated by Ibsen's skill in making stage action appear to proceed from the emotional logic that determines inner realizations. Sometimes the characters make their entrances as though answering a call. This is literally the case with Erhart in Act III. They wait outside doors, ready to make an entrance, as though they themselves were the inner outcome of the dialogue. Contrary to his usual habit, Ibsen does not tell us much about their pasts, social positions, or homes (except for the Borkmans). Many of them are drawn to fit the situation, with just the amount of clarity needed to reflect what they are supposed to reflect.

In any case, Ibsen largely dispensed with causal and motivational factors. On the whole, the dramatic action moves smoothly and uninterruptedly from one confrontation to another. The handling of the endings of the acts is largely responsible for this. No time elapses between the acts; they merge into one another. One act takes up the action and dialogue exactly where the previous one left it. For example, the conversation between Borkman, Ella, and Gunhild that begins in

Act II and is continued in Act III would not be inter-
rupted if it were to follow its inner logic. But the
rooms and the characters' movements in these rooms
or between one room and another express what is going
on in their minds. Thus, there is a break—whose only
purpose is to change the scene. The acts should really
not be separated by a curtain and an intermission. One
room ought to lead into another; the setting for Acts
III and IV should include the open winter landscape.

Voices and steps are heard offstage, evoking imaginary rooms and crystallizing into figures and dialogi-
cal situations almost as this happens in dreams. Whole
passages of dialogue seem to be subject to the law of
dreams. The self splits to represent an existential situation as it does in dreams. For instance, when Gunhild
is talking to her twin sister, Ella, she is also confronting
the nobler and "richer" self that resides within her as
a potential. In the same way, Borkman confronts the
carefully hidden shabby side of his own self in the
figure of Foldal. Ibsen's late work has what has been
described as a hermetic, monological character. The
loose, dreamlike handling of interconnections and
transitions may indicate that in the figures and situations of this play he was dealing with his own life.

In Act I, Ibsen begins his exposé of Borkman's life
by showing its consequences: the sterility he has
inflicted upon the lives of Ella, Gunhild, and Erhart.
Then he shows Borkman in his prime, at the height
of his career. We see how his troll-like existence, never
achieving self-mastery and incessantly torn between
the magical past and the technological future, has
destroyed Gunhild's existence; she is dragging out her
life in an attempt to live down her "shame" and restore
the past. In her, Borkman's vision of humanity and
the future has shrunk to a vision of the family and the
past. She has replaced utopia, which stimulates creativ-

ity and presses forward beyond the present, with a lost paradise for which she can only passively yearn.

Although all urge for progress (which Borkman himself once possessed, even though only in a troll-like form) is dead, wishful belief in magic lives on. Erhart is to "rise so high and shine so brightly that no one will remember the shadow his father cast upon [them]." "His life shall be so pure and high and bright that [Borkman's] years of burrowing in the dark will be wiped out!" These are the plans to which Gunhild hopes to get Erhart to commit his life, as she expresses them in the first and third acts. The similarity of phraseology shows how formalistic and narrow her imagination has grown, while the visual images prove that these are wishful dreams with which she brightens dark reality.

Gunhild has not merely condemned her own life to sterility but struck at the root of Erhart's existence, for she has failed in what should have been her life work of bringing up children to be "honest, upright people" (*The Master Builder*). Since she has charged Erhart with the "mission" of wiping out his father's dark life through his own bright purity, it is important to her to retain "a mother's power over her son." Thus, her conduct, too, is dictated by a lust for power but is not ennobled by the brotherly love that inspires Borkman. She sacrifices the man of the future to her past-dominated wish to see the Borkman who went to his ruin in bankruptcy return in a purified manifestation. Being committed to a mission produces in Erhart the same kind of split that caused his father's downfall. On one hand, it forces him into a lack of freedom and will; on the other hand, it makes him arrogant. Erhart himself brilliantly diagnoses this conflict, which moves him out of his center, in the charge that he is being subjected to something between pampering and idolization.

Trained to subservience, Erhart, too, cannot exclude magic from his path. Gunhild and Ella, both elderly women, wage the same kind of life-and-death fight over him they waged over Borkman when they were young, except that this time it is a spectral fight. Erhart is to become a purified or "undivided" Borkman who will make amends for the bungled past. But this is a fight for a specter born of their wishful thinking. True, Gunhild concludes the ruthless struggle with confident words: "Erhart himself shall choose between us." But choice, symbol of self-mastery, is as far beyond Erhart as it was beyond his father, who says himself, "I had no choice."

"Luring arms" also hold Erhart fast, though in his case it is not the lure of the mine that makes him unfree but an erotic tie. By depicting Fanny Wilton, the voluptuous and wealthy demimondaine whom Erhart follows to seek happiness in the south, as a sort of Nordic Circe, Ibsen has strikingly brought out Erhart's erotic enslavement. She threatens to lay a spell on him to make him follow her. The sleigh in which she takes him away from his parents' house has bells whose sound is repeatedly evoked in the fourth act. The ringing of the metal, which lured Erhart's father out of his inmost self, reechoes in the "tinkle of the silvery bells" and the "sound of the silver bells."

Thus, the lifelines of Gunhild and Ella twice intersect over men. When they were young, both of them tried to center themselves in a man who had never found his own center. They repeat this again, late in life. This indicates that Borkman's dividedness and incompleteness splits what should grow together in unity. (This is why it is only "over the dead man" that the twin sisters can hold out their hands to one another again.) Here Ibsen introduces a bold innovation in the motif of the man caught between two women, which he pursued from play to play. By making the women twins, he points back to the unity that has been split into duality, divided into two antithetical manifestations. It also becomes clear that the dialogue is fundamentally monologue.

In Gunhild, we recognize the dark face of Borkman, sometimes distorted into the features of a troll. She is driven by a desire for power and honor; she does not hesitate to use other people as stakes to gain her own advantage; and she cannot shake off the past. In Ella, however, Borkman's "extravagant" generosity has realized itself. She reflects his earlier readiness to help other people to achieve happiness and prosperity. It is true that even Ella is not immune to the temptation of letting Erhart make amends for the past by filling the vacuum of her loneliness, soon to be ended by death. But she derives her claims from love alone, expects sacrifice only out of affection. She is not interested in the power and honor that could come to her through Erhart. She wants Erhart himself, his "whole soul," his "undivided heart," so that she may grow to wholeness herself. Unlike Gunhild, she finally sets him free to live his own life, to seek the happiness he strives for.

Gunhild and Ella, two "shadows" pulling apart, who have never found the connection to their center, end in failure. Gunhild pays for her selfish craving for power and honor in helplessness and a lifetime of shame. And Ella's unselfish generosity in lavishing her money on the Borkman family's happiness bears no fruit. Like Borkman in his prime, she "throws money out of the window." Selfishness and unselfishness are not reconciled through Borkman; he does not achieve self-mastery.

Gunhild receives her husband and her son from Ella's hands. She never possesses either of them. While Ella has to give up the man she loves and her foster son to the power impulse, Gunhild, who owes her possession of her husband and son to Borkman's troll-like acquisitiveness, is never legitimized in her ownership. Everything is taken from her as arbitrarily as it was given to her. In the end she lives entirely on her sister's "kindness and charity." Ella's riches cannot be plundered by Borkman's dark covetousness, and this is quite natural, because she embodies the one component of his life which has a future—the willingness to devote his own assets to the wellbeing of others.

Step by step, Ibsen leads us back into the past by tracing the course of Borkman's life. With a sort of inevitability John Gabriel Borkman himself materializes in the second act out of Gunhild and Ella, who stand for his past and his split purposes. From what was formerly the great gallery of the house, his aimless pacing back and forth and the strains of the "Danse Macabre" make themselves heard above the two women's discussion. In the first scene of this act Foldal's regular evening visit with Borkman obscurely parallels the conversation between Gunhild and Ella. Foldal, Borkman's boyhood friend, who has been a petty clerk since he too went bankrupt, is nonetheless still submissive to John Gabriel. In his youth he wrote a tragedy, which he never succeeded in publishing.

Like Borkman, Foldal is a failed creator of human characters who never uses his creative gifts to perfect those nearest to him, who has never had an eye for the unredeemed and the unmatured except in the case of the spirits from the depths of the earth. But the connection between these two men is more complex still. While Gunhild and Ella inexorably quarrel over the meaning of existence, the two bankrupts devote themselves to upholding one another. The sole function of their relationship is to bolster, evening after evening, their images as, respectively, an exceptional person and a talented writer. The destructive effects of this curious friendship are not, however, very different from those of the enmity between the twin sisters.

Borkman can believe in Foldal only as long as Foldal believes in him. He has good reason, for Foldal embodies the poetic element in Borkman: the impotent, passive imagination that fills his mind with "fantasies" and "empty dreams" lends the botched past the brightness of the future and alienates him from reality and the present. Since Foldal sees him as larger than life, Borkman is not aware of the shabbiness of his runaway imagination. In Foldal we see an imagination at work that has been made "destitute" by Borkman. After the bankruptcy Foldal had "practically no choice" and was forced into poverty, with the result that his wife and children now despise him. He is therefore always prone to take dreams of the future for the reality of the present.

Through these two friends Ibsen reveals another dichotomy in Borkman: the power-hungry man of reality and the helpless dreamer. For eight years Borkman has kept Foldal a prisoner in the faded Empire-style gallery where he could see himself as the Napoleon of banking. Foldal, who, because he is still destitute, is ready to see wishes and dreams as reality, has held Borkman back from the creativity he has within him. So Borkman, too, has his twin. Here again there is dialogue that serves as a façade for monologue. For years Borkman has been talking to himself and has therefore disregarded reality. To this extent, he is right in saying that the person he sinned against is himself.

That Foldal's fantasies are far removed from reality is also evident from the way he, like Borkman, declares that the women around him are inadequate and seeks the "woman of nobility," who exists "somewhere far away," instead of perceiving her close at hand in the person of Ella Rentheim. Foldal, obsessed by his failure, sees life exclusively in the outdated images of rise and fall. For years Borkman fails to face the obvious comical and farcical aspect of life, which makes humanity "go round and round in a circle." There can be no fresh start, only the farcical continuation of the outdated game. His supply of life-sustaining lies is inexhaustible. The young people, Erhart and Frieda, take up the dreams at the point where they have lost their value to the older generation. They lose themselves in new fancies (Erhart at the lawyer Hinkel's) and let themselves be lured off toward distant paradises.

On the winter evening of the drama the two lifelong friends fall out because Borkman casts some doubt on Foldal's sense of reality. The mistrust grows and destroys the bond whose purpose was to keep doubt at bay. The ceremonial routine, in which Borkman had found refuge day after day, is exploded; the monologue has run down. Borkman is assailed by scruples, qualms of conscience, self-doubt; his unsureness immediately assumes physical shape in Ella Rentheim. Or should one say that a premonition of Ella's return draws him out of his self-deception and away from Foldal, much as Ella forced Erhart to reveal himself? Be that as it may, it is once again clear enough that events are determined by the logic of inner processes.

Since the trial Borkman and Ella have never met face to face. Eight years in prison and eight years of

self-imposed captivity lie between them. The judgment, as well as the sentence, is repeated twice over.
Ella echoes the judge's verdict: "Criminal!" Now,
however, the discussion concerns not Borkman's offenses against right and the law of the land but his deep
inadequacy and his "great, unforgivable sin": "You
killed love in me! You are guilty of double murder!
The murder of your own soul and of mine!" For the
first time he has to admit the guilt, which a short time
ago in talking to Foldal he disguised as "trouble over a
woman." Ella now learns that Borkman sacrificed love
to his insatiable desire for power.

Borkman, who, up until a few moments before, was
"unshakably sure of himself," begins to waver; he can
no longer fight off his suspicions about himself: "I don't
know any more which of us is right." He agrees to let
Ella, who is the last of her line, adopt Erhart, sensing
that his family's only hope of a future is for Erhart to
become her heir and inherit her fortune. At this
moment Gunhild, who has been lurking outside the
door, enters.

Act III continues the discussion downstairs. Space,
time, and people have become mobile. Borkman
leaves the gallery, where time has turned to space and
stagnated. Ella has restored him to the continuity of
his life's history. Gunhild and Erhart are milestones in
its course. He must confront them before he can rise
again to the height he reached in his early manhood.
But both deny him the future. For Gunhild, he is dead.
All she is concerned with is to annul his life, "to draw
the veil of oblivion over John Gabriel Borkman." She
builds the future on her son.

Erhart, who wants to break loose from "pampering
and idolization," from the chains of the past and fantasies of the future, is committed to the naked present.

He counts on his youth. The past does not matter to him any more than Fanny's husband does. He does not worry about the future or what may happen later. He has no wish to impose goals or meanings on life; all he wants is life itself, to feel the "tingling warmth" of its vitality. The desire for happiness becomes uncompromising. Which woman is to fulfill it and "whether it lasts or doesn't last" are immaterial to him. However the dice may fall, he will "manage." Everything is "unstable."

So Erhart joins the dance of life. Frieda, Foldal's fifteen-year-old daughter, is one of the party leaving for the south. Some day she will replace Fanny, who is seven years older than Erhart. And since Erhart, like his father, is susceptible to incantations, no one is better qualified to succeed the bewitching Fanny. Frieda "has music in her bones" and—with the ambivalence of everything that lures men—plays dance tunes as well as she plays the "Danse Macabre." And so between these two twinlike women Erhart will ruin his life, just as his father ruined his. Everything has grown flatter. Instead of striving upward, Erhart yearns for distance. But the prospects of a future are no greater. Nevertheless, for the time being, the three living characters defy the legend of the dance of death by fighting free of the three dead ones.

Borkman, who had made a brief attempt to win Erhart for himself, is meanwhile preparing for a new life. Like a Prometheus who has cast off his chains, he wants to start afresh, leaving dreams behind, and to atone for his past through a present and future wrested from reality. Like many of Ibsen's characters, he mistakes the end for a new beginning because it stimulates him to find new illusions to replace his old ones. So Borkman and Gunhild (who rushes after Erhart) throw open the door to the outside world—the icy mountain landscape of the fourth act. Both of them are still seeking their lost youth.

Erhart has already fallen back. Gunhild soon falls back too, locking herself up in the empty house. But before Borkman can again set foot on the first landscape he ever knew, he must finally shake off Foldal, who can never let go of a dream and embroiders even the most sober reality into a fairy tale. Borkman is already far ahead of him in truth. Foldal, who has been run over by Fanny's speeding sleigh, limps after him. He believes every word of the letter Frieda has left him, which says that she will leave next day under the protection of Fanny Wilton, accompanied by a capable teacher, to continue her musical education. He is not at all upset when he learns that he is too late to see Frieda again. "So my little poetic talent . . . was transmuted into music in Frieda. After all, I have not been a poet for nothing. For now she has the chance of going out into the great wide world, which I once so yearned to see."

Since Foldal lives in the belief that his empty youthful dreams will be fulfilled in his daughter, he will never be convinced that it has all been in vain. Refusing to face the chilling, deathly recognition that youthful illusions produce no reality, he turns homeward. The tragicomic element often present in the final scenes of Ibsen's characters is distributed between the two lifelong friends. Foldal's exit is touching and comical. Borkman's fate, when he falls victim to his illusions, is horrifying and tragic. Although Borkman's life is fully explained by the interplay of shabbiness and greatness, Ibsen meant the contrast to indicate that he finally transcends the pitiful weakness in his character.

After Borkman has reviewed "his whole wasted

life" and the existences that have withered away in its shadow, he begins the ascent to the "steep slopes and heights" from which he once dreamed of "a kingdom of industries" extending far into the vast landscape. He, too, has shown himself incapable of founding Ibsen's utopian "third empire," of uniting in a higher uniformity the chthonic, pagan past, nourished by the forces of nature, and the Christian vision of a future mankind dominated by brotherly love.

Ibsen has grown more skeptical since Peer Gynt returned to the land of his youth and found redemption in Solveig's love, which made him whole. Borkman too has returned, but no such transformation and blessed destiny awaits him. It is true that Ella follows him, but she cannot draw him up to her level, although her treatment of the Borkman family has given ample proof of her loving readiness to restore men to their freedom, truth, and primal nature. Borkman's early vigor flares up again. Once more an industrial empire stretches before his prophetic eyes. But the vision of this old, decrepit man, growing stiff with cold, makes it even clearer than before that the empire is a spectral one, coveted because of his obsession with power and prestige but not actively pursued through the efforts of a free will, to which the future belongs. The truth that he will "never make a triumphal entry into his cold, dark kingdom" forces itself upon him before "a metal hand" clutches at his heart. Since Borkman had always followed a dark urge and never moved forward into the epoch of civilized humanity, even in death he belongs to the realm of nature.

If we compare *John Gabriel Borkman* with *Peer Gynt*, we see how Ibsen refined his talent for compression. At the center of both plays is a tremendous personality lost in unproductive dreams. The one is a boisterous, uninhibited play of early manhood, which ambitiously attempts to deal with a journey round the world; the other, a play of old age, a retrospective survey, which, through the skillful interweaving of past and present, can unroll a whole life in the space of one winter evening.

When We Dead Awaken

Ibsen described this three-act drama, published at Christmas, 1899, as a "dramatic epilogue." This overt repudiation of the inner form of the traditional play is suggestive. In this subtitle the word "dramatic" does not define the genre but merely qualifies the species—epilogue. The word "epilogue" indicates that this play does not stand isolated.

Whether or not Ibsen intended *When We Dead Awaken* to set the seal on the nineteenth century or on his own *oeuvre* or even on his intellectual existence, the term "dramatic epilogue" assigns a chronological and autobiographical value to it. It forces us to see it from a certain viewpoint. Either we look down from this peak upon the spiritual landscapes of the earlier plays or we look up from them to what Thomas Mann called "this celestial work of old age." To be sure, the play, in which the sculptor Rubek and his former model Irene von Satow review their lives, is from the dramaturgical point of view a résumé. This is true of almost every play Ibsen wrote during the years when he was one of the leading figures in world literature, but in no other case did he feel obliged to offer any explanation of the form. This suggests that the term "epilogue" has nothing to do with the leading characters but seeks to make a basic final statement on the fruitlessness of human life as the play portrays it.

Once again we must ask how a dramatic action based on concentration and precipitation can be derived from an epilogue that summarizes the past across a gap of bitterness, an epilogue that is obviously a monologue by Ibsen himself spoken through the mouths of his characters. Whether he was really aiming at concentration is questionable. It is true that he restricts the action to three days. The three acts span a "mild summer morning," a "summer afternoon, toward sunset," and an "early summer morning" before sunrise. But in Acts I and II he places the action in vast natural settings—the "open, parklike space in front of the hotel" and an "immense plateau bare of trees" near a sanatorium—while Act III is played against the background of a "wild, fissured mountainside." Ibsen has departed radically from the milieu of the small-town middle class or the conservative landed gentry in which he has hitherto placed his interlocked characters. Here he has transferred them to open country (although the natural panorama has something slightly stagey about it).

The background, which towers like a pyramid, its steeply rising planes suggesting eternity, is in keeping with the growing tendency of Ibsen's late plays (which reaches its peak in *When We Dead Awaken*) to deal with pure humanity rather than social man. Social oppositions do occur but in a signficantly changed form, namely, in the order of values in which men are ranked according to their natural nobility of soul. This is illustrated by the way Rubek and Irene are contrasted with Ulfheim, a land owner and troll-like huntsman, and Maia, Rubek's wife. These landscapes, wide open to the dimensions of breadth and height, give Ibsen the vast scope demanded by the sweeping style of his old age, which loosely sketches the unity of the multitudinous. He handles plot and dialogue with "a majestically sclerotic weariness" (to quote Thomas Mann), without stiffness but with a sovereign sense of correspondences. Private concerns are subdued by the natural panorama. Impulses, gestures, and words are tired and heavy, broken and hesitant; then they become feverishly emotional and high-pitched, with an exaggeratedly shrill, exultant sensuality. But the excitement is largely limited to the third act. The tone of the two earlier ones is one of irony, mockery, and reservation, and this gives the dialogue a dragging, cagey quality—a certain unreality, as though much remains unsaid.

Hans E. Gerlach, who is translating Ibsen into German, points out that Acts I and II are more than twice as long as Act III, and that almost exactly at midpoint they both shift from the Rubek-Maia situation to the Rubek-Irene situation. To protect Ibsen's reputation as a precise dramatic technician, he suggests performing the play in five acts. But this is to overlook the fact that this "epilogue" is not constructed out of sequential, discrete plot units but on the spiral principle of incessant recapitulation, which focuses more and more sharply on the past, constantly casting new and more revealing light on it—at least in the first and second acts.

Another reason for Ibsen's choice of this vast natural setting, free from social implications, is the opportunity it offers to bring out more strikingly the parallelism of the two stories, which may converge in infinity. Obviously Acts I and II are intended to stand as a pair against Act III, because they show Rubek standing squarely between the two women as if between two

possibilities. In the last act the two couples have
formed and the women confront each other on stage
instead of appearing successively. Movements change
from horizontal to vertical, become more decisive, take
on a dramatic accent, strive for finality. Ibsen, then,
was not primarily seeking concentration, but he
brought out the dramatic character of the epilogue by
arranging it, from a higher point of view, in a pattern
of parallelisms. To deepen these correspondences fundamentally, he did not dissect his characters psychologically in his usual fashion but, as the Austrian
theater critic Alfred Polgar said, drew them larger than
life.

To squeeze a dramatic action out of what Thomas
Mann called "this craftsman's ghastly whispered confession," this "late—much too late—declaration of love
of life," Ibsen wrote his "epilogue" as the drama of
the artist afflicted with remorse for a botched life. This
is how Rubek sees himself. This is the image, hewn in
stone, that he wants to leave to posterity. Yet this
remorse, which painfully mulls over the past, only
needs to be diverted to the right channels to make even
the most misspent life appear redeemable. This opportunity comes to Rubek through his meeting with Irene.

As has been noted, from beginning to end of the
play two streams of remorse seem to flow in opposite
directions. Remorse turns man toward the past; but
since remorse is endowed with the power of eradicat-
ing the guilty act, it also lifts him above his own history. By getting beyond the past, one gets a better
view of it. Only when we realize this do we understand
that the play, which explicitly concentrates on the
past, is striving in the very same process toward the
higher world—as the stage settings so clearly indicate.

The play opens with one of Ibsen's favorite themes—
the return to the land of youth. Here we have yet

another variation on the theme of repetition, rejuvenation, and new beginnings. Once again Ibsen is dealing with the drama of the man who *becomes* the dramatic hero in his quest for his own truth. Since the focus of the play is on nonvisual inner developments, Ibsen uses the technique of making outer events comprehensible as inner ones and objectivizing spiritual happenings.

Arnold Rubek, a famous elderly artist whose works are exhibited in museums all over the world, had left Norway some five years before the play opens, after marrying Maia, a much younger woman with a keen appetite for life. His life, when he married her, was already a failure, because he was really in love with Irene, his first model. Ibsen chose a sculptor, whom he deliberately apostrophizes as "poet," as the subject for his final, definitive judgment of the artist—that dilettante in life who glimpses man's utopia but never realizes it. "Just a fool! Just a poet! . . . drifting about between false heavens on rainbows of lies"—Nietzsche's words might have been written of Rubek. All his strength is devoted to wresting from the stone the statue he refers to, with pseudoreligious solemnity, as his "life's work." The work symbolizes Judgment Day.

When he meets Irene, he finds "the fountainhead of his achievement," for he can envision the awakening from the sleep of death only in the form of a "young, unsullied woman." She becomes his symbol of the human being of the future, the citizen of the "third empire," illuminated by the "splendor of transfiguration," awakening to his truth. He achieves it, however, by "poetic subterfuge" (to quote Nietzsche). Man who has risen to self-consciousness is seen as an apotheosis. Divine potentialities are attributed to him. This makes it all the more painful to see how man's desire to grow is betrayed and blocked. First, art is posited as abso-

lute. It uses the sacred, a vital element in man's development, to advance itself. The work of art calls upon
man "as for an act of worship." Man has solemn dignity
only so long as he serves art. Thus reduced from an
end to a means, he is estranged from his utopian
divinity.

Furthermore, Rubek has falsified the myth of man as
he envisages him. He suppresses Ibsen's realization
(and Ibsen knew his Hegel) that the road leading
man to his promised self-realization is a dialectical
one, that the power of the spirit is only as strong as
its expression, its depth only as deep as its courage in
expanding and losing itself in its interpretation. In the
finished statue Rubek was deluding himself that man
would find himself again, in Goethe's words,
"unchanged . . . in the higher, freer, happier region,"
free of "our earthly life's experiences," without having
to "put away anything ugly and impure." (I shall
return later to Ibsen's allusion to the closing scene of
Faust, Part II.)

Rubek sacrifices his love for Irene to the celebration
of art, the sanctification of the work. He is thus forced
into an aesthetic aloofness, the "imperative of comple-
tion" that Thomas Mann attributed to Ibsen himself.
When the statue is finished, Irene leaves him because
he "no longer had any use" for her. Their separation
was not a matter of distance. "Suddenly and unexpectedly," she vanished, as though into death. She was
simply "extinguished." Suddenly disappearing without
a trace, she was "nowhere to be found," transported
into another dimension, spirited away. Her being
became inaccessible.

Rubek, in his loneliness, comes to realize something
that Ibsen himself recognized only late in life, when he
had attained a higher view of reality: self-realization is
not achieved through the sovereign power of the indi-

vidual but solely through the synthesis of the male and female principles, the synthesis of the powerful, creative man and the erotic, "extravagant" feminine nature. Irene held the key to his figures and visions. She was the muse who opened all that was locked up within him. After she left him, he plunged from the sacred region of art into a desert of emptiness and loss of self. Rubek falls from apotheosis into the flatlands of reality. His artistic style changes decisively. Giving up lofty symbolism, he develops an unmasking style in which he creates ambiguous and cryptic, yet apparently realistic, portrait busts. But there is something mysterious about these portraits. "Behind and beneath the surface they are horse faces . . . donkey muzzles and dog skulls . . . pig snouts and sometimes brutishly staring oxen." Still, even in debasing man from likeness to the angels to animality, Rubek misses his truth.

Now art no longer adumbrates the man of the future in surreptitious idealization but follows the "experiences of earthly life." And Rubek alters his master work to bring out the tellurian rather than the solar aspect of man. "And the plinth grew . . . and on the bigger plinth I placed a segment of the curving earth, bursting open. And from the fissures of Earth swarm people with faintly animalistic faces . . . as life had taught me to see them." The figure of the transfigured young woman no longer stands in the center. Rubek has portrayed himself in this group as the remorseful man weighed down with guilt, imprisoned forever in the hell of his despair.

Such are the depths into which life has plunged Rubek when he meets Irene again in a dreary Norwegian spa, after a conversation with Maia that begins in veiled animosity and boredom with one another and soon develops into ironic taunts. Their meeting is foretold in a dreamlike nocturnal vision. Rubek, unable to

sleep, goes to the window and sees "something white—
a light figure" moving through the park, closely followed by a second figure which is "quite dark, like a
shadow." Unrecognized—a substantial form or a mere
impression of whiteness?—Irene glides past. It is as
though she had to tear herself loose not only from the
surrounding shadows but also from self-destroying
estrangements from reality. When she appears the next
morning as the Lady in White, in a stiff, statuesque
pose, with her eyes half-closed, Rubek recognizes her
immediately. The shadow is individualized into a
black-robed deaconess who follows Irene about, "keeping her piercing brown eyes incessantly fixed on her."

The descent into Hades has taken Irene deeper into
the valley of death than Rubek has ventured. Her existence having been debased by that which Rubek subjected her to, she adopted the model's posture to which
he had reduced her: "I appeared in cabarets. Stood
naked on a revolving pedestal. Posed as a naked statue
in *tableaux vivants*." The annihilating realization that
Rubek no longer had any use for her love, that he had
"sinned against her inmost nature," led her to engage
in casual affairs with a series of men. Two of them she
married—a South American diplomat and a Russian
from the Urals by the name of von Sadow—antipodes
suggesting the confusion that drives her about the face
of the globe.

Yet so untouched is Irene at heart by these debase-
ments, so foreign are they to her nature, that she still
dresses in virginal, bridal white—a promise that the
pure, unsullied quality that Rubek saw as her essence
is still immaculate. But hatred for the male principle
caused her to take the lives of the diplomat and the
Russian. Her desire for revenge, symbolized by the
knife she carries with her at all times, even in bed, is
accompanied by self-hatred. As she says herself, she is

dead, not only because Rubek murdered her but also
because in her desperate readiness to lead the life of
a person whose moral self-esteem has been destroyed
she has "extinguished herself." Her self-hatred is also
revealed in her confession that she has defied her destiny and killed the children in whom she might have
been reborn, "murdering them with passion . . . long,
long before they were born." The destruction of her
nature, which was destined for transfiguration, ends in
madness. She suggestively describes the asylum to
which she was confined as a sepulcher and the time
she spent there as a time of death.

Irene is the last in the long procession of Ibsen characters whose painful fate it is to survive themselves,
to outlive their own deaths. We see how far her alienation from herself has progressed in the way she objectifies her inner biography in places and people that are
beyond her control. She identifies her soul with the
marble statue of the transfigured woman and keeps
telling Rubek that she wishes to make a pilgrimage to
the place where her soul lies buried. She projects the
guilt feelings, which imprison her in the living death
of self-rejection, upon the deaconess, whom she accuses
of practicing magic, thus trying to hypostatize her own
feeling of being divided. When she says, "She changed
herself into my shadow," she is groping toward understanding, making the deaconess (who watches over her
semirecovered patient with a straitjacket handy in case
of sudden emergencies) a symbol of her imprisonment
in the Hades of unexpiated self-betrayal. This is why
she says that "some fine sunny morning" she intends to
kill the deaconess, whom she calls a witch.

The magical projection of her guilt prevents Irene
from seeing her "resurrection" as a moral act. She must
think the deaconess has a hold on her from behind,
from some hellish pasts, as if her attendant, whom she

constantly interiorizes, were holding her down in self-concealment and self-denial. In fact, she is personifying in her an omnipresent sense of guilt, which is independent of place or time. "Even when she's not with me, she keeps a close watch on me," she says. "Wherever I may be, she never takes her eyes off me." While Irene thinks she can make contact with Rubek only when she can elude the deaconess's imaginary spell for a moment, she is actually accessible to him at the moments when she frees herself from her own delusions. Furthermore, the more clearly Rubek, who holds the key to her expiation, emerges from the lost past and becomes a living presence to Irene, the more inevitable it seems that she will ascend out of the "sepulcher" and be transfigured.

A cryptic passage points to associations of this kind. When Rubek confesses his guilt, Irene starts up "with a cry of deliverance," exclaiming: "At last! . . . There! Now I'm free of them! For this time they've let me go!" The word "they," which is not to be explained by grammar or by the context of meaning, suggests the Furies. If this association is tenable, then Irene's disturbed mind must see the deaconess as a black-robed nineteenth-century goddess of vengeance, who will punish her for "self-murder" until she can free herself from self-hatred. This interpretation can stand only if it does not conflict with the deaconess's own stage reality independent of Irene.

Obviously, the sister, "who wears a silver cross on a chain on her breast," represents Christianity. Here we must recall an idea that occurs frequently in Ibsen's work, at least after *The Emperor and the Galilean*. The Christian principle does not surrender man to his boldest willing; it holds him down in self-contempt, denying him access to the "promised heights," the "higher, purer, happier regions" of self-realization, where the powers of light and the powers of darkness work together in higher uniformity. To symbolize Julian's assault on the imperial throne, from which he hopes to initiate a classical renaissance, Ibsen makes him break out of the dark vault of a Christian church toward Helios—day transfigured by the sun.

While Irene and Rubek struggle on "through the night and toward the light," freeing themselves from the stranglehold of the past by reliving it and breaking through to the present, beginning their lives anew through repentance and expiation, the scene shifts to a vista of sky and the rising sun. But before Irene and Rubek can come together again, they must bridge an abyss of distance and lack of forgiveness. The dialogue painfully and clumsily surmounts all the obstacles in its way—resignation, despair, mistrust, and hostility. Each time, Rubek has to turn away from Maia, who is falling ever more exuberantly under the spell of Ulfheim, the faunlike bear killer, toward Irene, who lurks behind him with her knife, eager to give vent to her hatred. There is no way of recapturing lost time. They cannot call it back; they can only sum it up so that their existence may be reborn out of past-entrammeled soullessness into the utopia of daylight, transfigured by being. Then perhaps some possibility of a future may be renewed, though not their youth.

To suggest the irrevocable flow of time, Ibsen even included a stream in the stage setting for Act II. Running diagonally across the stage, it separates Irene and Rubek at the beginning and end of their scene together. Sitting on the banks of this stream, they replay the past and their botched lives in the flat sequences of time. Scattering mountain azaleas in the water, Irene tears apart the blossoms of dreams that never unfolded and watches them drift away. Rubek throws leaves—his "ships"—after them, but they run aground.

They used to play games of this kind when they were young, but in those days Irene would choose water lilies, flowers that "shoot up from the very bottom," as Ibsen says in *Little Eyolf*. This was her way of forcing Rubek into the dimension of depth, where he could become aware of man's earthbound origin and tellurian nature. This nature is not to be transmogrified into a god like one by poetic subterfuge; it must grow beyond itself into transfiguration. But Rubek was not ready for initiation into the law of "die and become." The lily was poeticized into a swan, the leaf he attached to it became Lohengrin-Rubek's boat. And so the swan, symbolizing Irene's bridal purity, fulfilled its function of drawing the modern Lohengrin, who is not to be questioned about his terrestrial origins, toward the pseudoreligious Holy Grail castle of artistic genius. Considering the difficulties of "beginning life afresh," it is not surprising that Irene should be "taken" again by the deaconess at the end of the second act.

Act III takes place before a backdrop of mountain peaks towering toward eternity. The episodic undecisiveness of the slow-moving dialogue of the second act would be out of keeping with such a background. The third day is dawning, the day when the descent into Hades merges into resurrection.

Maia and Ulfheim, to whom the mountain heights are a region of primitive joy in nature, have spent the night in a hut. Ulfheim has persuaded Maia to go bear hunting with him and has tried to make her the prey— a bridal rape that hints at archaic states of the soul. But Maia, whose name relegates her to the world of appearance, does not resist for long. She thinks that by yielding to earthly experiences she will achieve "freedom—

real, genuine life." Ulfheim, who is in the habit of shooting his "best friends" (dogs) when they fall sick, knows death only as a physical phenomenon, the swift transition from exuberant life to lifelessness. He looks like a goat-footed faun, but he sometimes dreams of a princess who will release him from his bear hide and make him a prince again. Maia, however, cannot serve as a princess, and so, when a threatening storm breaks, they flee to the flatlands of reality.

On a scree at the foot of a slope they meet the other couple coming up. Rubek and Irene are oppressed by the knowledge that the "summer night," which might have been life because it would have given life the boon of light and darkness, is no longer within their reach. But they struggle on toward the peak from which, when they were both young, Rubek had promised to show Irene "all the splendors of the world." (For the third time Ibsen concludes a play with a reference to the final scene of Goethe's *Faust*, Part II.) Although her first love has returned to Irene, he is not restored to her in atonement. Once again her language glows ecstatically; her feelings flare up in youthful enthusiasm. But this is the euphoria of death. Through the mists that envelop their bodies like a shroud, they fight their way forward to their "marriage feast" in the "glittering glory of the light."

But the traces of the past are ineradicable. The couple is held fast to rough, earthly paths. Before they can "once drain the beaker of life to the dregs," the avalanche breaks loose and sweeps them down to the valley. The deaconess, who has followed them, has the last word. "Madame von Satow!" she screams, forcing Irene back into the very manifestation she was trying to escape. Then, with the words *"pax vobiscum,"* she speaks the last amen over the couple. To be sure, the couple did not want to lay their lives to rest in the *pax Christiana.* Rather (as intimated by the name Irene—the word *irēni* means peace in Greek) they wanted life to culminate in a peace that would afford them an existential fulfillment in the Greek sense.

STAGE PRODUCTIONS
IN AMERICA

The early productions of Ibsen in America foreshadowed the ambivalence with which Ibsen is regarded in this country to this day. On the one hand, there was not the typically American resistance to European artistic innovation. Many first American productions of Ibsen's plays were fairly contemporaneous with their European premieres; in fact, the world premiere of *Ghosts* took place in America (in Chicago, but given by a Norwegian company). On the other hand, the major early success of Ibsen here was a distorted version—*Thora*, a British version of *A Doll's House* with a so-called happy ending. In *Thora* the Nora figure returns to her husband at the end, thereby vitiating Ibsen's ideas.

By 1890 the American theater acknowledged the obvious importance of Ibsen as an innovator in handling serious current problems in contemporary set-

---

This chapter on the stage productions of Ibsen in America has been specially prepared for this American edition by Leonard S. Klein.

tings. And there were many productions of Ibsen in America during the next four decades. One of the early exponents of Ibsen was Minnie Madden Fiske, who, after a great success as Nora in 1894, played Ibsen's heroines again and again. The great Russian actress Alla Nazimova performed in the works of important European playwrights in America, thus enriching the cultural life of her adopted country. Nazimova played Ibsen roles for several decades; her interpretations included Nora, Mrs. Alving, Hedda, Hilda Wangel in *The Master Builder*, and Rita in *Little Eyolf*.

During the 1920s there were many important Ibsen productions. In 1924, Eva Le Gallienne began her long-term dedication to producing Ibsen. Blanche Yurka had a three-play Ibsen season in 1929. Perhaps most impressive during this period was a visit of Eleonora Duse to New York in 1923, during which she and her Italian company acted in *Ghosts* and *The Lady from the Sea*. Stark Young, one of the major drama critics of the time, was ecstatic in his praise of Duse in both roles. Discussing her interpretation of Ellida Wangel, Young felt that Duse's performance outshone *The Lady from the Sea* itself: "She enlarges the play until it goes beyond anything the author had imagined for it. . . ." (The consequences of this denigration of Ibsen were pernicious—however justified it may have been in this exceptional case.)

During the 1930s Ibsen's plays began to lose their popular appeal. The tightly knit dramaturgy was being challenged by looser forms, and the social themes lost their immediacy. (The universal themes had scarcely been understood anyway.) Thus began a period of neglect of Ibsen; the occasional revivals were greeted with condescension by the popular press. Flaws that should have been charged to performance and translation were attributed to Ibsen. It was not at all surprising that the misunderstanding of Ibsen's philosophy that led to the early *Thora* should again lead to rewritings. One such example was Thornton Wilder's modernization of *A Doll's House* (1937), in which Ruth Gordon had one of her first major successes.

Eva Le Gallienne, who spent the better part of forty years touring the country in the plays of Ibsen and other important modern dramatists, brought several of her productions of Ibsen (in her own very good translations) to New York in the late 1940s. Her staging of *John Gabriel Borkman* (1946, with Le Gallienne as Ella and Margaret Webster as Mrs. Borkman) was generally well received. But the play was woefully misunderstood (and condescended to) by the newspaper critics. They found fault with the play's last act, and their reasons supporting this criticism showed a total lack of sensitivity to the meaning of the play.

In 1948 Le Gallienne brought productions of *Hedda Gabler* and *Ghosts* to New York. Unlike the *Borkman*, both of these productions suffered from bland interpretations. Not surprisingly, more of the blame was put on the plays than the productions. A reaction atypical only in its extraordinary crassness was the headline of the *Journal-American* review of *Hedda Gabler*: EVA SHOULD TAKE IT BACK TO THE MUSEUM (February 26, 1948). In reviewing *Ghosts*, the newspaper critics were quick to gloat about their observation that the play "could not have been composed after the discovery of penicillin" (Howard Barnes, in the *New York Herald Tribune*, February 18, 1948). Robert Brustein, an ardent defender of Ibsen, in discussing a 1961 production of *Ghosts* in the *New Republic*, made the point that congenital syphilis, undetected until its final phase, does *not* respond to penicillin. He then took the newspaper critics to task for their blind self-importance: "Still fixed on Oswald's unfortunate malady, a contemporary review can nevertheless be confidently expected to consist less of discussions of the play than of unsolicited testimonials to Sir Alexander Fleming and his discovery of penicillin."

In 1950 Arthur Miller had a major success with his adaptation of *An Enemy of the People*. The obvious appeal of Ibsen's play to Miller was its treatment of issues similar to those pervading the McCarthy era. This instant relevance was grasped (and loved) by the middlebrow Broadway audience. Brooks Atkinson called the Miller version "a vast improvement" on the original (*New York Times*, December 29, 1950). What this vast improvement consisted of was a simplification of the play, so that all the irony and humor were lost; what remained was a black-and-white confrontation of the two brothers. The production, staged by Robert Lewis, was strengthened by principals who could project with intensity the straightforward Miller dialectics: Frederic March (Dr. Stockmann), Morris Carnovsky (Peter Stockmann), and Florence Eldridge (Mrs. Stockmann). A 1971 revival by the Repertory Theater of Lincoln Center also benefited from a strong cast. This time, however, more critics recognized the loss of Ibsen's complexity in Miller's version.

As if in response to the success of Miller's *An Enemy of the People*, two major stagings of Ibsen plays were presented in New York in 1951. The first was *Peer Gynt*, the only Ibsen play written before *A Doll's House* with any significant stage history in America. The production was directed by Lee Strasberg (of the Actors Studio) and featured an unlikely cast including John Garfield (Peer), Mildred Dunnock (Aase), and Karl Malden (Button-molder). The production did not hold together at all; but again the major blame was directed at the play. The low state of Ibsen's reputation among what Eric Bentley has called the "Broadway intelligentsia" was never more apparent than in the following comment by Brooks Atkinson: "Without Grieg there does not seem to be much vitality in this symbolic yarn. . . ." (*New York Times*, January 29, 1951). The other Ibsen revival of 1951 was also poorly cast—*The Wild Duck* at the City Center. This time Mr. Atkinson told us that "Ibsen's craftsmanship is all-thumbs today" (*New York Times*, December 27, 1951). I choose Atkinson's remarks because he was then the most prestigious and influential newspaper critic; his reactions were unfortunately typical.

The poor quality of the productions and the hostile reaction to Ibsen by the popular press made Ibsen an unviable commodity on Broadway. From 1951 to 1971 the major Ibsen productions were the two given by the so-called experimental Phoenix Theater—both of them unsuccessful. One, Oscar Homolka's 1955 staging of *The Master Builder*, starring himself and his wife, Joan Tetzel, was so underplayed that it left the major dramatic critic Eric Bentley "angry at the sight of capacities unused." For Bentley, this production illustrated the reasons for the unpopularity of Ibsen since the 1920s: "If you emasculate an author, you can scarcely be surprised if ignorant persons declare him a eunuch from way back."

The 1960 Phoenix production of *Peer Gynt*, directed by Stuart Vaughan, failed for an opposite reason—being too bombastic. Robert Brustein found that the play was obscured by the production: "The Phoenix production never betrays the slightest hint that *Peer Gynt* has an intellectual content, a consistent theme, or, for that matter, any interest at all beyond histrionic sweep."

When David Ross began an Ibsen cycle at his tiny Fourth Street Theater, there was hope that he might repeat with Ibsen the limited success he had had with

Chekhov in the 1950s. The first play, *Hedda Gabler* (1960), was partly successful, mainly because of the interesting Hedda of Anne Meacham. But the two following productions—*Ghosts* in 1961 and *Rosmersholm* in 1962—were so bad that Robert Brustein was burning with rage: "I am just about ready to swear out writs of injunction—the first one going to David Ross, enjoining him to stay away from Ibsen."

After a decade of almost total neglect, Ibsen was resurrected once again in 1971, this time—at last—with real success. Patrick Garland directed Claire Bloom in both *Hedda Gabler* and *A Doll's House*. *Hedda Gabler* was at least illuminating, although the quiet iciness of Claire Bloom's Hedda seemed to transfer too much attention to the buffoon Tesman. The production of *A Doll's House* was a revelation to those who had given up all hope that Ibsen could be presented well in this country. From the bird chirpings she makes at the beginning to please Torvald to the famous slamming of the door, Claire Bloom's Nora was worthy of being called definitive. And the supporting cast was uniformly excellent. Although some critics seized on instant relevance and started talking about Women's Liberation (as if this were the only reason for a revival), the timeless dilemmas of Nora and Torvald were there on stage for those who wished to see them.

BIBLIOGRAPHY

SELECTED ENGLISH TRANSLATIONS
OF THE PLAYS

Brand. Translated by Michael Meyer. Garden City,
N.Y.: Doubleday, 1960.

The Collected Works of Henrik Ibsen. Translated by
William Archer. 11 vols. New York: Scribner's,
1906–07.

A Doll's House and Other Plays. Translated by Peter
Watts. Baltimore: Penguin, 1965.

An Enemy of the People. An adaptation by Arthur
Miller. New York: Dramatists Play Service, 1951.

Ghosts and Other Plays. Translated by Peter Watts.
Baltimore: Penguin, 1966.

Ghosts and Three Other Plays. Translated by Michael
Meyer. Garden City, N.Y.: Doubleday, 1966.

Hedda Gabler and Other Plays. Translated by Una
Ellis-Fermor. Baltimore: Penguin, 1961.

Hedda Gabler and Three Other Plays. Translated by
Michael Meyer. Garden City, N.Y.: Doubleday,
1961.

The Last Plays. Translated by William Archer. New York: Hill and Wang, 1959.

The Master Builder and Other Plays. Translated by Una Ellis-Fermor. Baltimore: Penguin, 1958.

The Oxford Ibsen. Translated by James Walter Mc-Farlane and others. 5 vols. to date. London: Oxford University Press, 1960 ff.

Peer Gynt. Translated by Rolf Fjelde. New York: New American Library, 1964.

Peer Gynt. Translated by Michael Meyer. Garden City, N.Y.: Doubleday, 1963.

Peer Gynt. Translated by Peter Watts. Baltimore: Penguin, 1966.

Six Plays. Translated by Eva Le Gallienne. New York: Random House, 1957.

When We Dead Awaken, and Three Other Plays. Translated by Michael Meyer. Garden City, N.Y.: Doubleday, 1960.

The Wild Duck. Translated by Dounia B. Christiani. New York: W. W. Norton, 1968. (This edition includes background and criticism.)

The Wild Duck and Other Plays. Translated by Eva Le Gallienne. New York: Random House, 1961.

TRANSLATIONS OF OTHER WRITINGS

From Ibsen's Workshop. Translated by A. G. Chater. Vol. 12 of *The Collected Works of Henrik Ibsen.* New York: Scribner's, 1911.

Ibsen: Letters and Speeches. Edited by Evert Sprinchorn. New York: Hill and Wang, 1964.

CRITICISM

Bentley, Eric. *The Playwright as Thinker.* Cleveland: World Publishing Company, 1955.

Bradbrook, M. C. *Ibsen the Norwegian: A Revalua-*

tion. rev. ed. Hamden, Conn.: Archon Books, 1966.

Brandes, George. *Henrik Ibsen: A Critical Study*. New York: Benjamin Blom, 1964.

Brustein, Robert. *The Theatre of Revolt*. Boston: Little, Brown, 1964.

Downs, Brian Westerdale. *Ibsen: The Intellectual Background*. Cambridge: Cambridge University Press, 1948.

———. *A Study of Six Plays by Ibsen*. Cambridge: Cambridge University Press, 1950.

Fjelde, Rolf, ed. *Ibsen: A Collection of Critical Essays*. Englewood Cliffs, N.J.: Prentice-Hall, 1965.

Gosse, Sir Edmund. *Henrik Ibsen*. New York: Scribner's, 1907.

Grene, David. *Reality and the Heroic Pattern: The Last Plays of Ibsen, Shakespeare, and Sophocles*. Chicago: University of Chicago Press, 1967.

Knight, G. Wilson. *Henrik Ibsen*. New York: Grove Press, 1962.

Lavrin, Janko. *Ibsen: An Approach*. New York: Russell & Russell, 1969.

Lucas, F. L. *The Drama of Ibsen and Strindberg*. London: Cassell, 1962.

McFarlane, James Walter, ed. *Discussions of Henrik Ibsen*. Boston: Heath, 1962.

———, ed. *Henrik Ibsen*. Baltimore, Penguin, 1970.

———. *Ibsen and the Temper of Norwegian Literature*. London: Oxford University Press, 1960.

Meyer, Michael. *Henrik Ibsen: A Biography*. Garden City, N.Y.: Doubleday, 1971.

———. *Henrik Ibsen: The Making of a Dramatist, 1828–1864*. London: Hart-Davis, 1967.

Muir, Kenneth. *The Last Periods of Shakespeare, Racine, and Ibsen*. Detroit: Wayne State University Press, 1961.

Northam, John Richard. *Dividing Worlds: Shake-speare's The Tempest and Ibsen's Rosmersholm.* New York: Humanities Press, 1965.

Shaw, George Bernard. *The Quintessence of Ibsenism.* New York: Hill and Wang, 1957.

Tennant, P. F. D. *Ibsen's Dramatic Technique.* Cambridge: Bowes, 1948.

Valency, Maurice. *The Flower and the Castle: An Introduction to Modern Drama.* New York: Macmillan, 1963.

Weigand, Hermann. *The Modern Ibsen: A Reconsid-eration.* New York: Dutton, 1960.

FULL-LENGTH WORKS USED IN "IBSEN PRODUCTIONS IN AMERICA"

Bentley, Eric. *What Is Theatre?* Boston: Beacon Press, 1956.

Brustein, Robert. *Seasons of Discontent.* New York: Simon and Schuster, 1965.

Young, Stark. *Immortal Shadows.* New York: Hill and Wang, 1958.

INDEX